Lonsdale STUDENT WORKSHEETS

INTRODUCTION

- These student worksheets are intended to act alongside the corresponding revision guide to help reinforce your understanding and improve your confidence.

- Every worksheet is cross-referenced to "The Essentials of G.C.S.E. Double award: PHYSICS (Physical Processes)" Edited by Mary James.

- The questions concentrate purely on the content you need to cover, and the limited space forces you to choose your answer carefully.

> These worksheets can be used ...
>
> ... as <u>classwork sheets</u> where pupils use their revision guide to provide the answers ...
>
> ... as <u>harder classwork sheets</u> where pupils study the topic first, then answer the questions without their guides ...
>
> ... as easy to mark <u>homework sheets</u> which test understanding and reinforce learning ...
>
> ... as the basis for <u>learning homeworks</u> which are then tested in subsequent lessons ...
>
> ... as <u>test material</u> for topics ...
>
> ... as a <u>structured revision programme</u> prior to the exams.

- Remember to fill in your score at the bottom of each page in the small grey box ▢, and also to put your score in the 'marks' column on the contents page.

CONSULTANT EDITOR: JOHN TOWNSEND

© 1999 LONSDALE SRG. ALL RIGHTS RESERVED. NO PART OF THIS PUBLICATION MAY BE REPRODUCED, STORED IN A RETRIEVAL SYSTEM, OR TRANSMITTED IN ANY FORM OR BY ANY MEANS, ELECTRONIC, MECHANICAL, PHOTOCOPYING, RECORDING, OR OTHERWISE WITHOUT THE PRIOR WRITTEN PERMISSION OF LONSDALE SRG.

Lonsdale Science Revision Guides - Physics Double Award Higher/Special & Foundation Tiers

CONTENTS

Forces

Page No.	
4	Speed and Velocity
5	Acceleration
6	Interpreting Distance - Time and Velocity - Time Graphs
7	Forces
8	Force, Mass and Acceleration
9	Friction
10	Forces on Vehicles
11	Force and Pressure on Solids
12	Force and Pressure in Liquids
13	Force and Pressure in Gases
14	Hooke's Law
15	Moments
16	Centre of Mass

Basic Electricity

Page No.	
17	Static Electricity I
18	Static Electricity II
19	Charge, Current and Voltage
20	Electrolysis
21	Current, Voltage and Resistance
22	Resistance
23	Current - Voltage Graphs
24	Series Circuits
25	Parallel Circuits
26	Electrical Power
27	Paying for Electricity
28	Electricity in the Home
29	The Three Pin Plug
30	Fuses and Double Insulation
31	Earthing and Circuit Breakers

Electricity and Magnetism

Page No.	
32	Magnetism
33	Electromagnetism
34	Applications of Electromagnetism
35	The Motor Effect
36	The Direct Current Motor
37	Electromagnetic Induction
38	Applications of Electromagnetic Induction
39	Transmission of Electricity
40	Transformers

CONTENTS

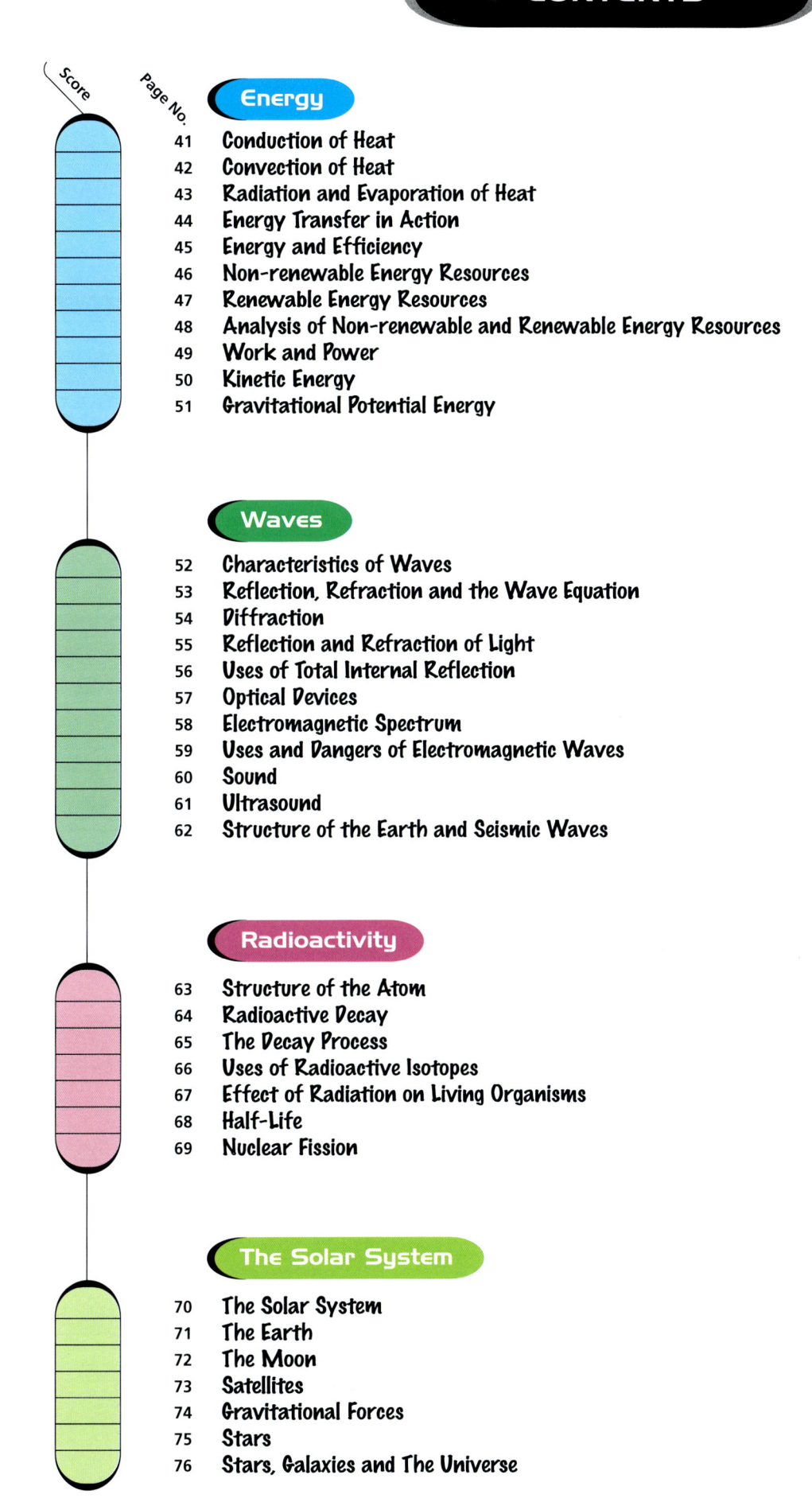

Energy

Page No.	
41	Conduction of Heat
42	Convection of Heat
43	Radiation and Evaporation of Heat
44	Energy Transfer in Action
45	Energy and Efficiency
46	Non-renewable Energy Resources
47	Renewable Energy Resources
48	Analysis of Non-renewable and Renewable Energy Resources
49	Work and Power
50	Kinetic Energy
51	Gravitational Potential Energy

Waves

Page No.	
52	Characteristics of Waves
53	Reflection, Refraction and the Wave Equation
54	Diffraction
55	Reflection and Refraction of Light
56	Uses of Total Internal Reflection
57	Optical Devices
58	Electromagnetic Spectrum
59	Uses and Dangers of Electromagnetic Waves
60	Sound
61	Ultrasound
62	Structure of the Earth and Seismic Waves

Radioactivity

Page No.	
63	Structure of the Atom
64	Radioactive Decay
65	The Decay Process
66	Uses of Radioactive Isotopes
67	Effect of Radiation on Living Organisms
68	Half-Life
69	Nuclear Fission

The Solar System

Page No.	
70	The Solar System
71	The Earth
72	The Moon
73	Satellites
74	Gravitational Forces
75	Stars
76	Stars, Galaxies and The Universe

SPEED AND VELOCITY

Forces

1. a) A car travels 120km in 3 hours. Calculate its average speed.

   b) An aeroplane flies 3600 km at an average speed of 1000 km/h. Calculate how long the journey takes.

   c) A 1500m runner takes 3 min 20s to complete a race. Calculate his average speed.

   d) A cyclist cycles at an average speed of 10m/s. Calculate the distance travelled in 3 hours.

2. Jim and Don were having an 800m race. Their times were recorded every 100m and the table below shows the results.

Time (s)	Distance run (m)								
	0	100	200	300	400	500	600	700	800
Jim	0	15	30	45	65	85	105	130	155
Don	0	20	40	60	80	95	110	125	140

a) On the same axes below draw both distance-time graphs.

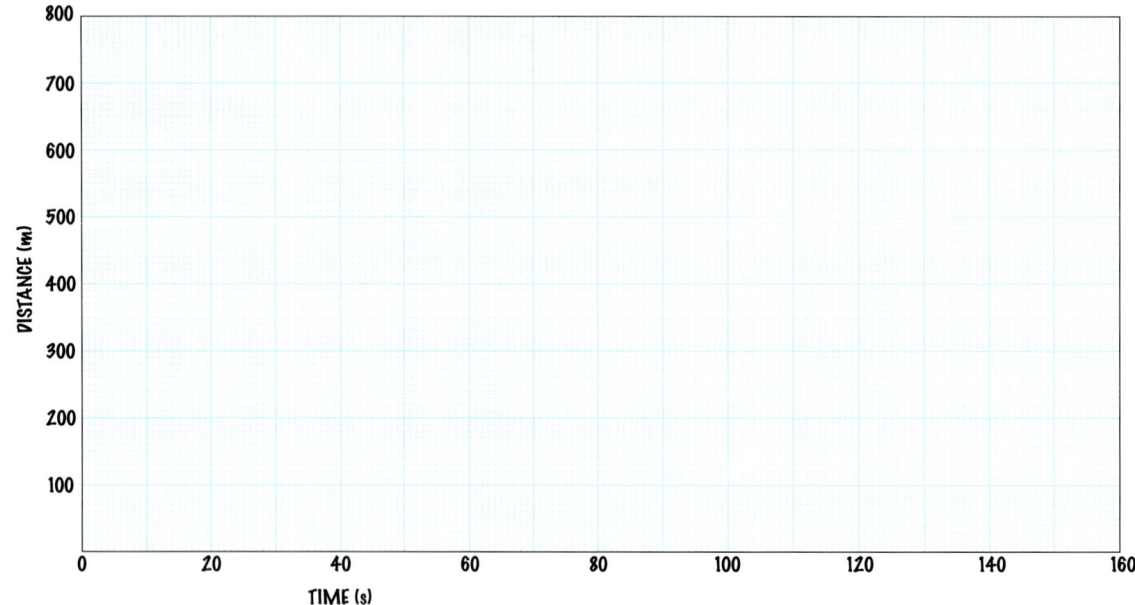

b) Between which two times was Jim's speed the slowest?

c) Between which two times was Don's speed the slowest?

d) Who won the race and by how many seconds?

ACCELERATION

Forces

1. a) A car accelerates uniformly from rest to a speed of 15m/s in a time of 5s. Calculate the acceleration of the car.

   b) A fighter plane lands on an aircraft carrier at a velocity of 40m/s, it is stopped in a time of 2s. Calculate the deceleration of the fighter plane.

   c) A train accelerates uniformly from rest at a rate of $2m/s^2$. If the train accelerates for 15s. Calculate the final velocity of the train.

   d) A car accelerates from a speed of 20m/s to 34m/s in 4s. What is the acceleration of the car?

   e) A cyclist at the top of a hill has a speed of 5m/s he then accelerates at $2.5m/s^2$ for 4s. Calculate his speed after 4s.

2. The table below shows the velocity and time of a motorcyclist which travels between two sets of traffic lights.

| Velocity (m/s) | 0 | 5 | 10 | 10 | 10 | 13 | 16 | 16 | 12 | 8 | 4 | 0 |
| Time (s) | 0 | 2 | 4 | 6 | 8 | 10 | 12 | 14 | 16 | 18 | 20 | 22 |

   a) Draw a velocity-time graph of the cyclist's journey on the axes below.

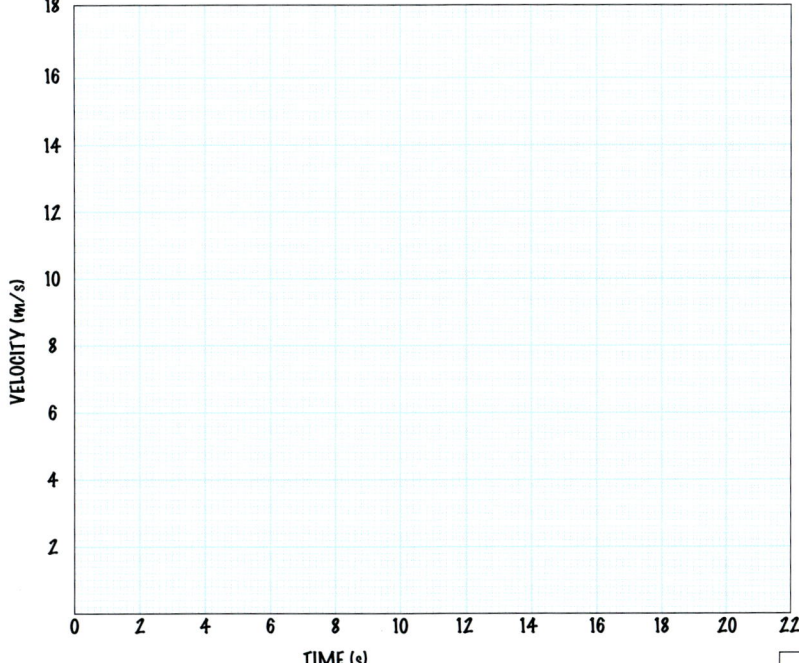

   b) Between which two times was the cyclist's acceleration the greatest?

   c) For how long did the cyclist travel in total at a constant velocity?

G.C.S.E. Ref: Page 10

INTERPRETING DISTANCE-TIME AND VELOCITY-TIME GRAPHS • Forces

HIGHER/SPECIAL TIER

1. The distance-time graph below is for Paula doing her shopping.

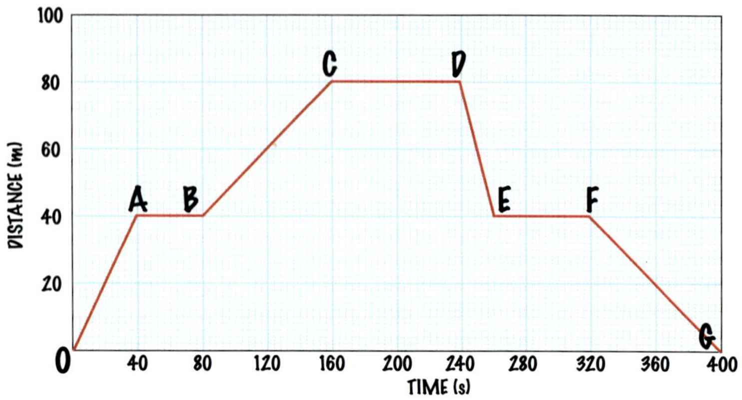

a) Describe the first four minutes of Paula's shopping trip.

b) In which region, OA, AB, BC, CD, DE, EF or FG was she travelling the fastest?

c) Calculate Paula's speed in the region OA, BC and DE.

OA:

BC:

DE:

2. The velocity-time graph is for a train moving from one station to the next.

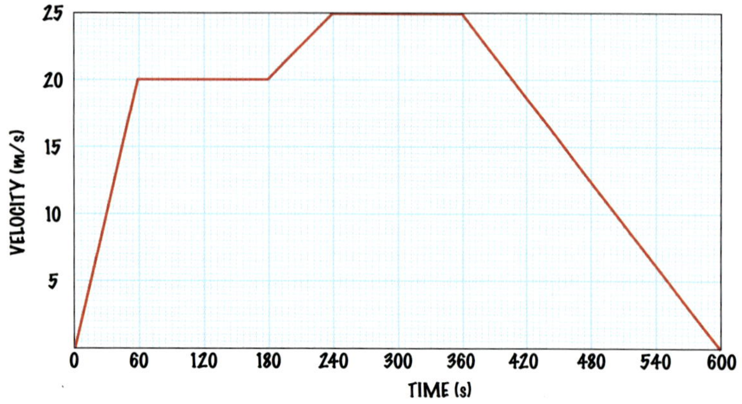

a) Describe the motion of the train.

b) Calculate the two accelerations of the train.

c) Calculate the deceleration of the train.

d) Calculate the total distance travelled by the train.

3. The velocity-time graph below is for a parachutist falling under the effect of gravity.

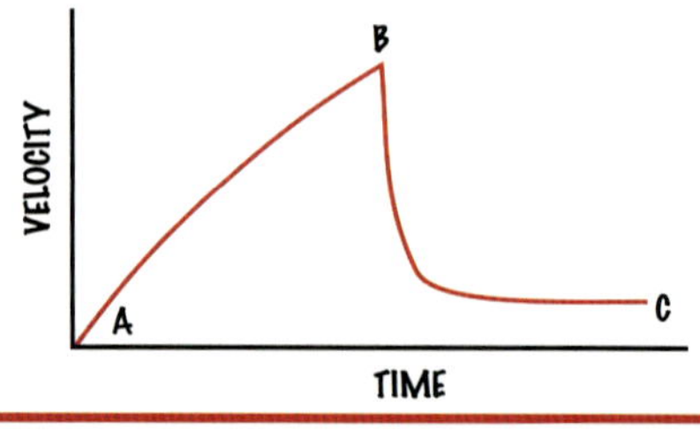

a) Describe the motion between A and B

b) Describe the motion between B and C.

FORCES

1. The diagram shows a car. The car is moving from left to right.

   a) On the diagram use arrows to indicate the direction of the following forces
      (i) the weight of the car
      (ii) the reaction force of the ground on the car.
      (iii) the driving force
      (iv) the resistive force.

   b) Describe the motion of the car if
      (i) the driving force and resistive forces are equal and opposite.

      (ii) the driving force is greater than the resistive forces.

      (iii) the resistive forces are greater than the driving force

2. A train is moving along a track. Describe the forces acting on the train when:

   a) the train accelerates.

   b) the train moves with constant speed

   c) the train slows down.

3. The diagrams show the forces acting on four different objects. The objects are all stationary to begin with. For each one

   a) work out the resultant force acting and
   b) state whether the object will move to the left, move to the right or remain stationary.

FORCE, MASS AND ACCELERATION • Forces

1. Diagrams A to F show the forces acting on three cars and three lorries.

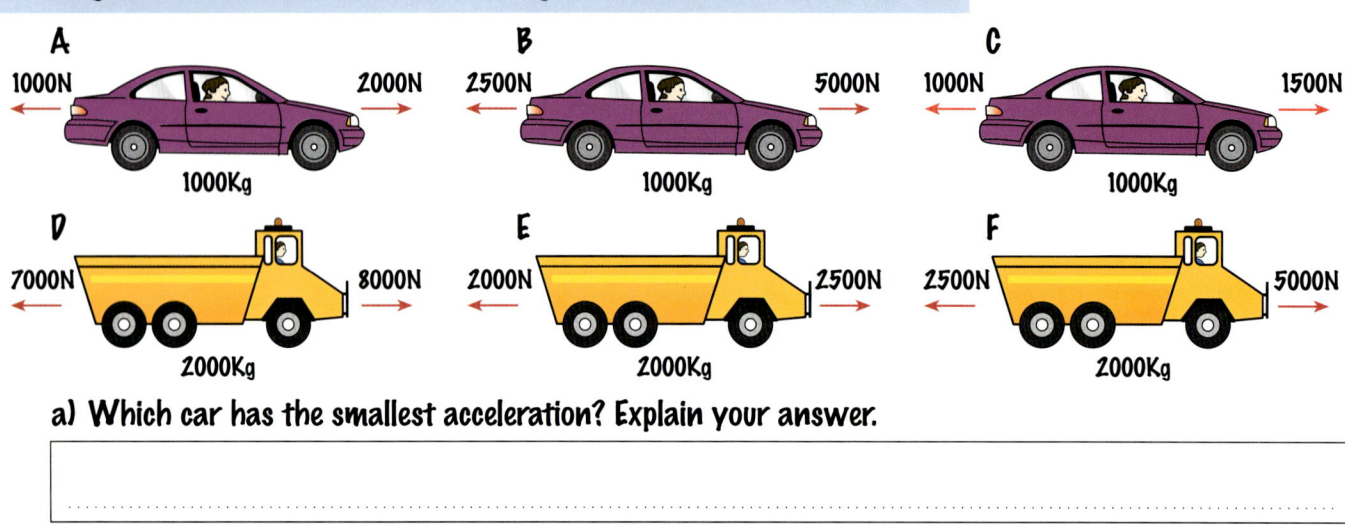

a) Which car has the smallest acceleration? Explain your answer.

b) Which lorry has the greatest acceleration? Explain your answer.

c) Will car B or lorry F have the greatest acceleration? Explain your answer.

d) Which two vehicles have the same acceleration? Explain your answer.

HIGHER/SPECIAL TIER

2. A car is moving along a road at a constant speed of 20m/s. The car produces a driving (push) force of 5000N.

   a) What is the value of the resistive force?

   b) The driver presses on the accelerator and increases the driving force to 7000N.

   (i) What is the resultant force (assuming the resistive force does not change) now acting?

   (ii) Calculate the acceleration of the car, if the mass of the car is 800kg.

3. A car of mass 1000kg is moving along a road. The resistive force (air resistance and friction) is 1000N. The car accelerates uniformly from 10m/s to 15m/s in 2s.

   a) What is the acceleration of the car?

   b) Calculate the force that produces this acceleration?

FRICTION

Forces

1. The drawing shows a skydiver of weight 700N.

   a) What happens to the weight of the skydiver as she falls?

   b) What is the value of the air resistance acting on the skydiver as she steps out of the plane?

   c) As the skydiver steps out of the plane she will fall and accelerate. Explain, in terms of the forces acting on the skydiver, why she accelerates.

   d) What will happen to the value of the air resistance as she falls?

   e) Explain why the skydiver will eventually stop accelerating.

   f) What is the name given to this velocity?

   g) Eventually, the skydiver will open her parachute. What effect will this have on the air resistance acting on her?

   h) What will happen to the velocity of the parachutist now?

2. Explain, in terms of the forces acting, why a car has a top speed?

3. The drawing shows the same cyclist in two riding positions. Explain why the top speed of the cyclist is different in position A compared to position B.

4. When man first landed on the moon some experiments were carried out. A hammer and a feather were both dropped together from the same height. Explain why they both hit the ground at the same time.

FORCES ON VEHICLES

1. A car is moving along a road at a speed of 15m/s. The drivers thinking time is 0.7s.

   a) Calculate how far the car will travel before the driver puts his foot on the brake.

   b) What factors affect his thinking time?

   c) What effect does an increase in thinking time have on

   (i) Thinking distance
   (ii) Braking distance
   (iii) Overall stopping distance?

2. Below is a velocity-time graph of a car having to make an emergency stop.

   a) What was the thinking time of the driver?

   b) How long did it take the car to come to a stop after the driver pressed the brakes?

   c) If the overall stopping distance of the car was 56m and the thinking distance was 16m what was the braking distance of the car?

   d) The driver then picks up three of his friends. State and explain how the following will change.

   (i) Thinking distance.
   (ii) Braking distance.
   (iii) Overall stopping distance.

3. Crumple zones, seat belts and air bags are all designed to increase safety in the event of a car crash.

   a) How do all of these safety measures reduce the risk of injury?

   b) If you were designing a car name 3 other safety measures you would introduce into your design.

FORCE AND PRESSURE ON SOLIDS — Forces

1. Use your knowledge of pressure to explain the following:

   a) 4x4 off road vehicles have wide tyres.

   b) Woodpeckers have strong pointed beaks.

   c) Drawing pins are pointed.

2. a) The crate shown has a weight of 600N. Calculate the least pressure that the crate can exert on the ground.

   b) In what position will the crate exert a pressure of $1600N/m^2$ on the ground. Show your calculation.

   (Crate dimensions: 0.5m × 0.75m × 2m)

3. A car weighs 10,000N. Each tyre has an area of $100cm^2$ in contact with the ground.

   a) What is the total area of tyre in contact with the ground?

   b) Calculate the pressure exerted on the ground?

4. a) A lorry weighs 320,000N. Each tyre has an area of $400cm^2$ in contact with the ground. Calculate the pressure the lorry exerts on the ground if it has 6 tyres.

   b) Another lorry weighs 420,000N. Each tyre has an area of $400cm^2$. Calculate the number of tyres the lorry has if the lorry exerts a pressure of $105N/cm^2$ on the ground.

G.C.S.E. Ref: Page 16 — Lonsdale Science Revision Guides - Physics Double Award Higher/Special & Foundation Tiers

FORCE AND PRESSURE IN LIQUIDS

Forces

1. Use your knowledge of pressure in liquids to explain the following:

   a) Deep sea divers have to wear very strong diving suits.

   b) The strength of a ship has to be greater the further it is under the water.

   c) A hole in a ship near the bottom is more dangerous than one near the surface.

2. a) Give two reasons why liquids are used in hydraulic systems.

   (i) (ii)

   b) An example of a hydraulic system is the hydraulic car brakes. When the brake pedal is pushed the brake pad pushes against the wheel disc. Explain why this system can be described as a force multiplier.

   HIGHER/SPECIAL TIER

   c) If the driver pushes on the brake pedal with a force of 200N and the area of the master piston is 2cm², calculate the pressure exerted on the brake fluid at the master piston.

   (i) What is the pressure transmitted through the liquid to the slave piston?

   (ii) If the area of the slave piston is 16cm² calculate the force exerted on the wheel disc?

3. The diagram shows a simplified hydraulic car jack.

   a) Explain how the hydraulic jack works.

   DOWNWARD FORCE
   Master Piston 'A'
   Slave Piston 'B'
   LIQUID UNDER PRESSURE

   b) If the weight of the car is 10000N calculate the downward force that has to be used to lift the car. The master piston has an area of 4cm² and the slave piston has an area of 80cm².

FORCE AND PRESSURE IN GASES — Forces

1. a) Explain what we mean by 'atmospheric pressure'.

   b) High flying aeroplanes have 'pressurised' cabins. Explain why.

HIGHER/SPECIAL TIER

2. Ahmed carried out an experiment to investigate how the volume of a fixed mass of gas changes with pressure. He kept the temperature constant throughout the experiment. The results are shown.

   a) Calculate the value of pressure x volume for each set of results.

Pressure (atm)	Volume (cm³)	Pressure x Volume
1	10.0	
2	5.0	
3	3.3	
4	2.5	
5	2.0	

   b) Plot a graph of the results on the graph paper opposite.

   c) What conclusion can be drawn from this experiment?

   (PRESSURE (atm) vs VOLUME (cm³) graph)

   d) A gas cylinder stores gas at a pressure of 10 atm. If the volume of gas in the cylinder is 1000cm³, calculate the volume the gas will occupy when released into the atmosphere (where the pressure is 1atm)

3. a) A weather balloon is released into the atmosphere. At ground level the volume of the air in the balloon is 400cm³. The pressure is 100000 N/m². If the balloon rises in the air to a height where the pressure is 25000 N/m² (assuming the temperature does not change), what is the new volume of the balloon?

   b) The balloon now changes its position and its volume becomes equal to 900cm³. What is the pressure at this position?

HOOKE'S LAW

Forces

1. Cathy and Jon carried out an experiment to find out how a stretching force affects the extension of a spring. The original length of the spring was 2cm. The table of results they obtained is shown below.

   a) Complete the table.

Load (N)	0	1	2	3	4	5	6	7	8	9	10
Length (cm)	2	3.1	4.0	4.9	6.0	7.0	8.3	9.8	11.6	14.0	17.0
Extension (cm)	0										

   b) Plot a graph of extension against load on the axes below.

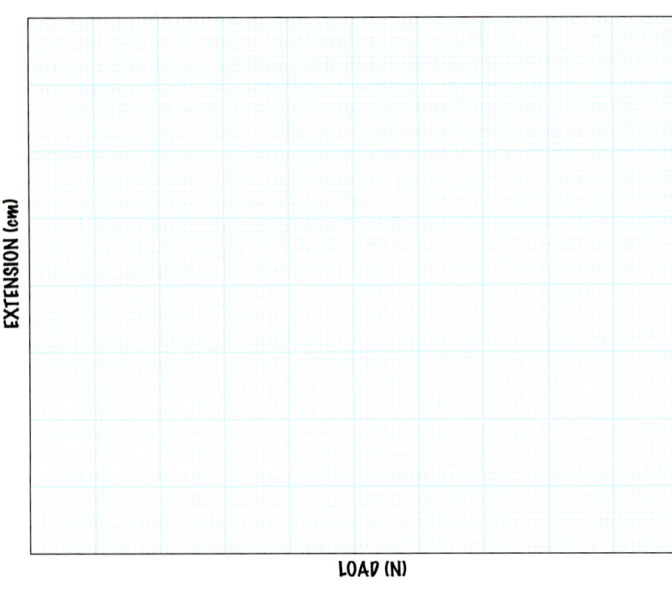

   c) On your graph label the elastic limit.

   d) What conclusions can you draw from this experiment?

   e) From your graph find:
   (i) the load that gives an extension of 7.5cm?

   (ii) the extension when the load is 2.5N.

   (iii) the length of the spring when the load is 3.4N.

2. A spring is 30cm long when it carries a load of 10N and 60cm long when it carries a load of 30N. Work out the following:

   a) the length of the spring with no load

   b) the length of the spring when it carries a load of 40N

   c) the extension of the spring when it carries a load of 55N

   d) the load required to produce an extension of 45cm

   e) the load required to produce a spring of length 105cm

3. A wire has an unstretched length of 60cm. When it carries a load of 10N its length becomes 61cm. The elastic limit is reached at a load of 50N.

   a) Estimate the length of the wire when the load is

   (i) 60N   (ii) 70N   (iii) 100N

   b) What could eventually happen to the wire if we continually increased the load?

MOMENTS — Forces

1. Explain the following:

   a) The pictures show two types of stapler. Why is stapler B easier to use?

   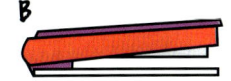

   b) Door handles are placed a long way from the hinges?

2. a) A mechanic applies a force of 200N at the end of a spanner of length 15cm. What moment does the spanner exert?

   b) The diagrams show six rulers, each one is on a pivot. For each one calculate the value of 'X'.

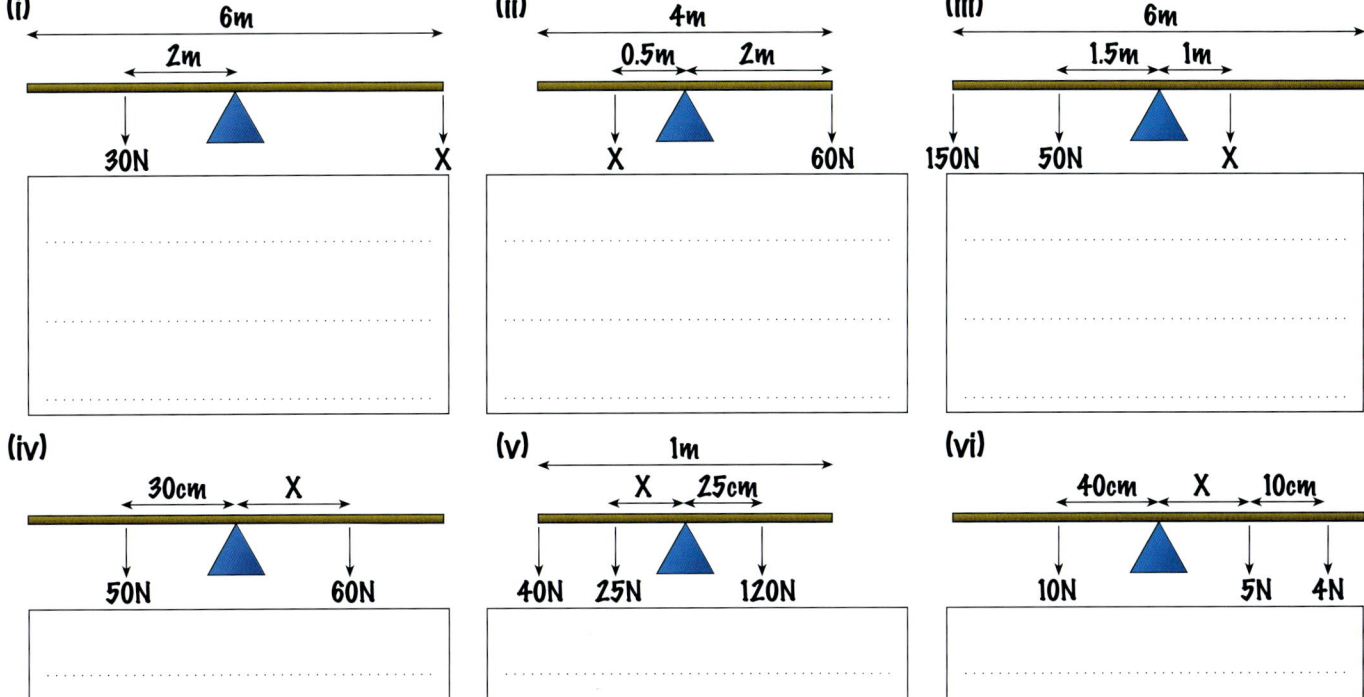

(i) 6m, 2m, 30N, X

(ii) 4m, 0.5m, 2m, X, 60N

(iii) 6m, 1.5m, 1m, 150N, 50N, X

(iv) 30cm, X, 50N, 60N

(v) 1m, X, 25cm, 40N, 25N, 120N

(vi) 40cm, X, 10cm, 10N, 5N, 4N

3. The diagram shows a very simplified picture of the roof of a stand at a rugby ground.

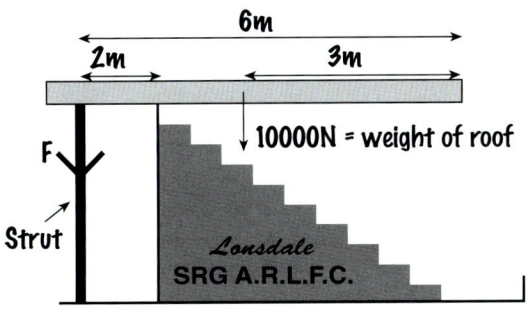

   a) Calculate the moment due to the weight of the roof of the stand.

   b) The strut has to exert a force on the roof of the stand to balance it. Calculate the size of this force.

CENTRE OF MASS

Forces

1. a) What do we mean by "centre of mass"?

   b) Describe an experiment to find the centre of mass of a piece of card (lamina). Draw a diagram to illustrate your answer.

2. The drawing shows three different wine glasses.

   a) Which is the most stable? Explain your answer.

   b) Which is the least stable? Explain your answer.

3. Explain the following:

   a) A bunsen burner has a wide heavy base

   b) A 4x4 vehicle has a wide wheel base

   c) People are not allowed to stand upstairs on double decker buses.

   d) A car becomes more unstable with a roof box.

   e) Racing cars are low with wheels wide apart

STATIC ELECTRICITY 1

Basic Electricity

1. Abida combed her hair. As she moved the comb away from her head some hairs were attracted to the comb.

   a) What has happened to the comb to make it attract the hairs?

   b) If the comb is held above some dry tissue paper, what will Abida notice?

2. Tony carried out an experiment. He charged a perspex sphere by rubbing it with a cloth. The sphere gained a positive charge. He then charged an ebonite rod with a piece of fur. The fur gained a positive charge.

   a) Explain how the sphere gained a positive charge.

   b) What charge did the ebonite rod gain? Explain your answer.

   c) Tony then suspended the perspex sphere as shown. He had hold of the insulating thread at all times.

   (i) Explain why Tony kept hold of the insulating thread in this experiment.

   (ii) State what would happen to the sphere if the ebonite rod was brought up close to it without touching.

   (iii) State what would happen to the sphere if the piece of fur was brought close to it without touching.

3. Bicycles can be painted using an electrostatic paint spray. The paint is given a positive charge.

   a) What charge should the bike be given? Explain your answer.

   b) What is the advantage of using this method?

   c) Describe one other use of electrostatics in everyday life.

STATIC ELECTRICITY II

Basic Electricity

1. Diagram (i) shows a metal dome of a Van De Graaf generator.
   The dome is charged so that it gains a positive charge. The dome is then earthed (diagram ii).

   a) Explain how the dome discharges?

   (i)   (ii)

   b) The dome was then given a negative charge. It was then earthed.
      Explain how the dome discharges now.

2. Lightning is caused because clouds become highly charged up. Lightning is a massive spark.
   Explain, in detail, how the charge gained by clouds is discharged to give lightning.

3. Whenever Seamus gets out of his car on a dry Summer's day he gets an electric shock as soon as he touches the car door.

   a) Explain why?

   b) Alisha suggests that Seamus gets a piece of conducting material like the one shown. She says this will prevent him from getting a shock.
      (i) Why must this be touching the ground?

      (ii) Explain how it will help to prevent Seamus getting a shock

4. Describe a situation where a high potential difference can lead to a potentially fatal situation. Suggest ways in which the problem can be prevented.

CHARGE, CURRENT AND VOLTAGE — Basic Electricity

1. The diagram shows an electrical circuit.

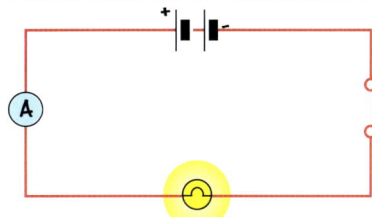

   a) Mark on the diagram the direction of conventional current. Label it 'current'.

   b) Show on the diagram the flow of electrons. Label this 'electrons'.

HIGHER/SPECIAL TIER

2. a) The circuit above is switched on for 60 seconds. The ammeter reading is 3A. Calculate the charge that flows in this time.

   b) If the circuit is switched on for 30 seconds and a charge of 450 coulombs flows calculate the current.

3. In the circuit shown the cells provide a potential difference of 6V. A current of 0.25A flows for 5 minutes.

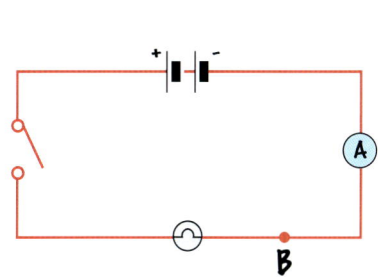

   a) Calculate the charge that passes point B in these five minutes.

   b) Calculate the energy transferred in the circuit in the five minutes.

4. A current of 5A flows in a circuit. A total charge of 2000 coulombs passes a point in the circuit. Calculate how long the circuit has been switched on for.

5. The diagram shows a simple circuit. The circuit is switched on for 100s. In this time the lamp produces 200J of energy. The potential difference provided by the cells is 20V.

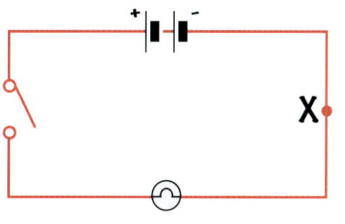

   a) Calculate the charge that passes point X whilst the circuit is switched on.

   b) Calculate the current that flows in the circuit.

ELECTROLYSIS

Basic Electricity

1. The diagram shows the apparatus used for the electrolysis of copper chloride.

   a) Explain how a current flows through the copper chloride solution.

   ....
   ....
   ....

   Copper Chloride →

   b) A current of 1A will deposit 1 gram of pure copper on the negative electrode in 20 minutes. Suggest TWO ways in which 5g of copper could be obtained using this apparatus.

   (i) ....

   (ii) ....

   HIGHER/SPECIAL TIER

   c) If a current of 10A flows through the apparatus for 60 minutes:

   (i) Calculate how much charge is transferred between the positive and the negative electrode.

   ....

   (ii) What mass of copper is deposited on the negative electrode?

   ....

   d) The potential difference across the electrodes was 12V. Calculate the energy transferred.

   ....

2. Copper which is to be used for electrical wires must be very pure. One way of making pure copper is by electrolysis. The positive electrode is impure copper. The negative electrode is pure copper. The diagram below shows the arrangement used.

   -ve

   +ve

   a) A current of 2 amps flowing for 30 minutes will deposit 2g of copper.

   (i) Calculate how much charge flows through the solution.

   ....

   (ii) How much charge flows through the solution to deposit 20g of copper?

   ....

   (iii) During electrolysis it took 120 minutes to deposit 20g of copper. Calculate the current flowing.

   ....

   (iv) If the potential difference across the electrodes was 24V, calculate how much energy was transferred.

   ....

CURRENT, VOLTAGE AND RESISTANCE — Basic Electricity

1. The circuit diagrams show several circuits (each cell and bulb are identical).

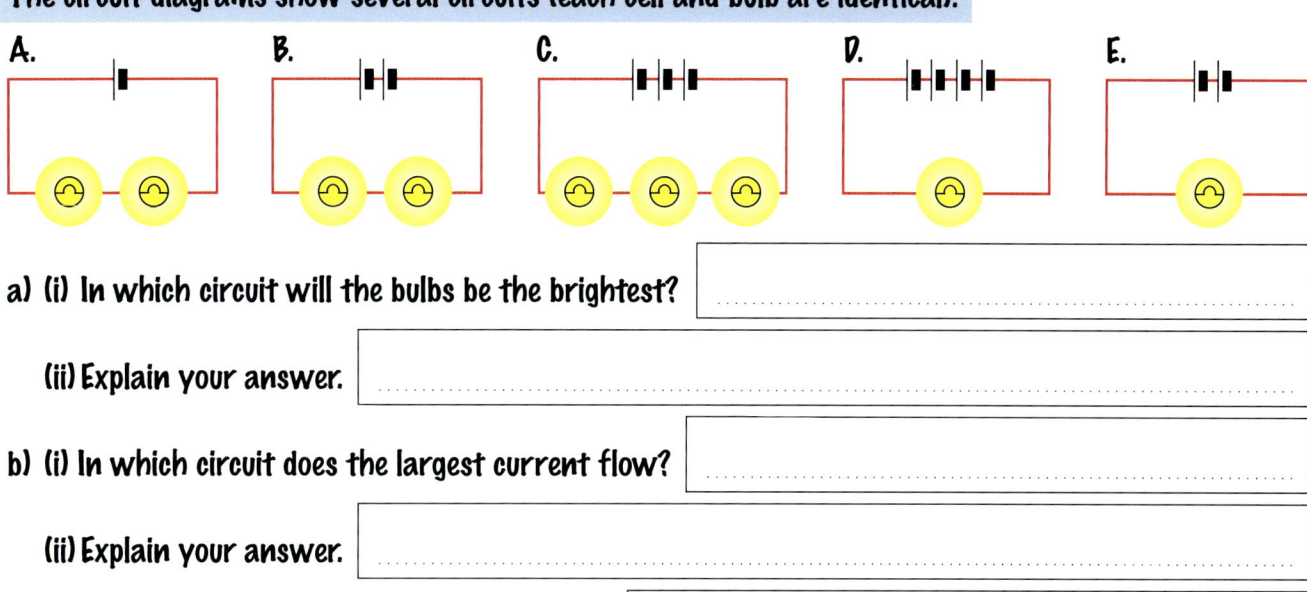

   a) (i) In which circuit will the bulbs be the brightest?

   (ii) Explain your answer.

   b) (i) In which circuit does the largest current flow?

   (ii) Explain your answer.

   c) (i) Which circuit has the greatest resistance?

   (ii) Explain your answer.

   d) (i) Which circuit has the highest potential difference?

   (ii) Explain your answer.

2. The circuit diagram shows three batteries in series with a lamp.

   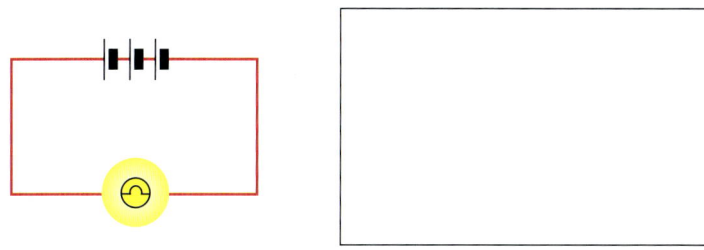

   a) (i) Redraw the diagram and add an ammeter.

   (ii) What does an ammeter measure?.

   b) Now add an electrical component to your diagram to measure the voltage across the lamp. What is the name given to this component?

3. An electric current passing through an electrical device has a heating effect.

   a) Name THREE common electrical devices that make use of this.

   (i)   (ii)   (iii)

   b) The diagram shows a 'ring' on an electric cooker.
   (i) Explain why the ring gets hot when an electric current flows through it.

RESISTANCE

Basic Electricity

1. The circuit below was used to measure the resistance of a fixed resistor.

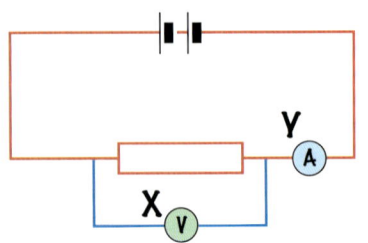

   a) Name the component labelled Y

   b) If the first reading on the Voltmeter is 6.0V and the Ammeter is 1.5A

   (i) Calculate the resistance of the resistor.

   (ii) If the voltage is increased to 9V what current would now flow through the resistor?

   (iii) A different resistor was placed in the circuit and the current flowing when the voltage is 6V is 0.2A. Calculate the resistance of the resistor.

HIGHER/SPECIAL TIER

2. The resistance of the thermistor was found over a range of temperatures. The table below shows a set of results.

Resistance (Ω)	Temperature (°C)
3000	0
1800	10
1250	20
900	30
600	40
500	50
350	60
300	70
300	80

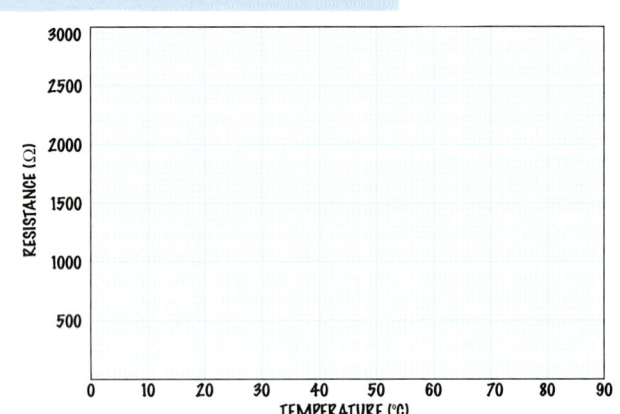

   a) Plot a graph of the results.

   b) Describe as fully as you can, what happens to the resistance of the thermistor as the temperature changes.

   c) If the potential difference (voltage) across the thermistor was 12V. Calculate the current flowing through the thermistor at a temperature of 40°C.

   d) If the readings of the Ammeter and Voltmeter were found to be: Voltmeter = 12V Ammeter = 0.0096A

   (i) What is the resistance of the thermistor?

   (ii) At what temperature were these readings taken?

CURRENT - VOLTAGE GRAPHS

Basic Electricity

1. A student decides to investigate how the current through a filament lamp changes as the voltage across the lamp is changed.

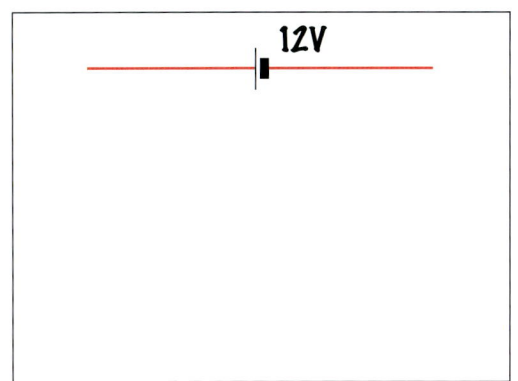

a) Complete the circuit diagram to show how she should set up the circuit.

b) The results she obtained are shown in the table below.

Voltage (V)	0.0	2.0	4.0	6.0	8.0	10.0	12.0
Current (A)	0.0	1.0	1.4	1.7	1.9	2.1	2.2

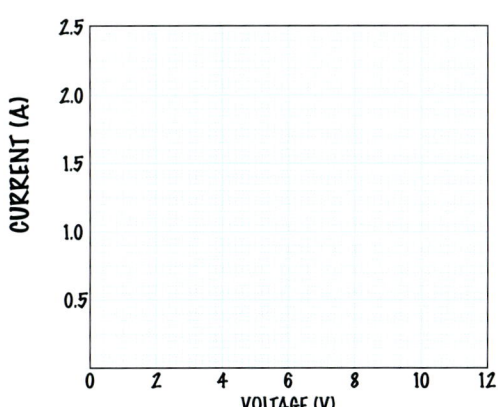

c) Plot a graph of current against voltage.

d) Use your graph to calculate

   (i) the resistance of the lamp when the voltage is 3V.

   (ii) the resistance of the lamp when the voltage is 9V.

e) What happens to the resistance of the lamp as the current passing through it increases? Explain your answer.

2. Another student used the circuit shown above to find out how the current through a diode changes as the voltage across it is changed. The graph drawn shows the results.

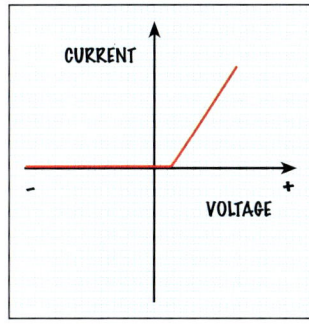

a) Describe how the current changes as the voltage changes.

b) Sometimes batteries are inserted the wrong way round into an electrical appliance. Explain how a diode can be used to stop the device from being damaged.

SERIES CIRCUITS

Basic Electricity

1. In the space provided draw a circuit diagram to show three cells connected in series with three lamps.

2. a) In the series circuits below all the components are identical. By using the information in circuit (i) write in the missing values of current and voltage in circuits (i) to (iv).

(i) 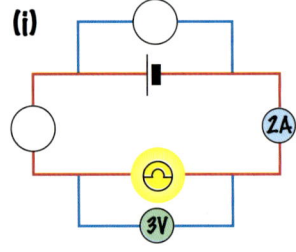   (ii) 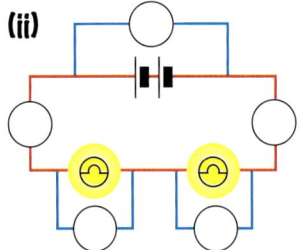   (iii) 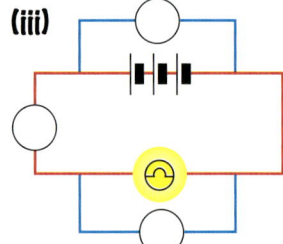   (iv)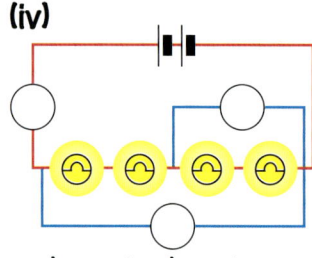

b) For each one draw a circuit diagram including ammeter and voltmeter readings if each bulb now has twice the resistance.

3. In the following circuits each resistor has a resistance of 10Ω. For each circuit calculate the total resistance and write in the missing values of current and potential difference.

(i) 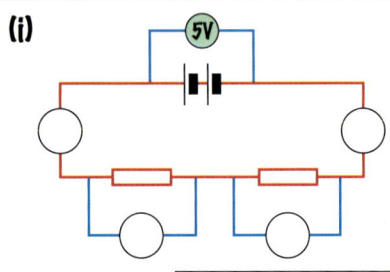   (ii) 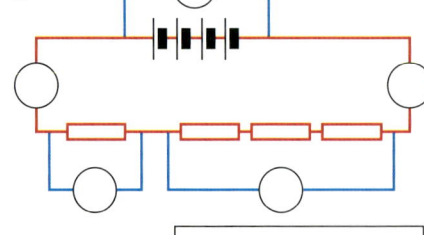   (iii)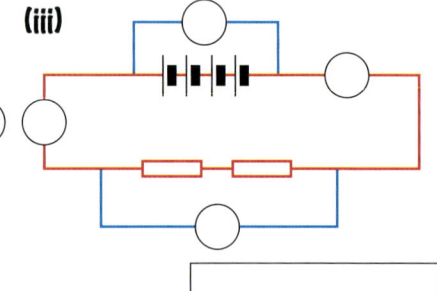

Resistance = ...   Resistance = ...   Resistance = ...

4. For the following circuits write in the voltage across each resistor and calculate the total resistance of each circuit.

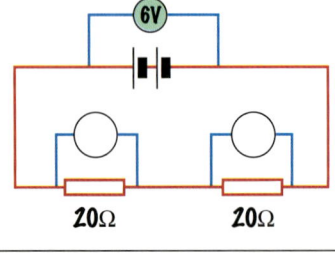   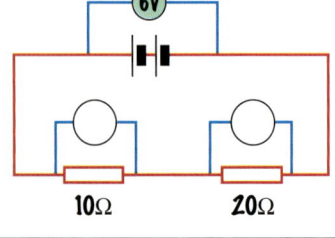   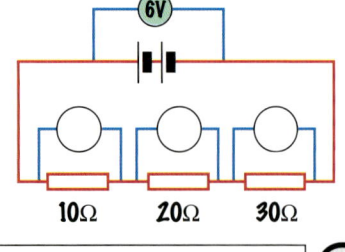

24 — Lonsdale Science Revision Guides - Physics Double Award Higher/Special & Foundation Tiers — G.C.S.E. Ref: Page 31

PARALLEL CIRCUITS

Basic Electricity

1. For the following parallel circuits write in the missing values of current and voltage.

   (i) 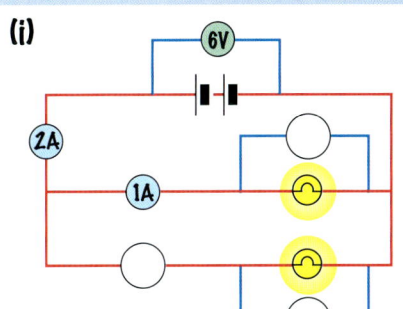   (ii) 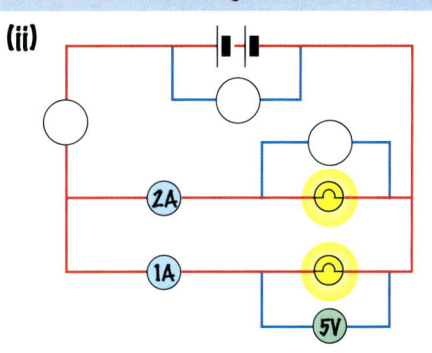   (iii)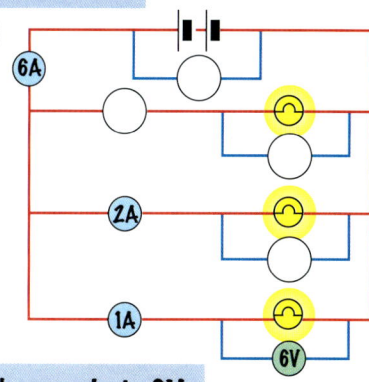

2. The circuit shown was set up. All the lamps are identical. The voltage of the supply is 6V.

   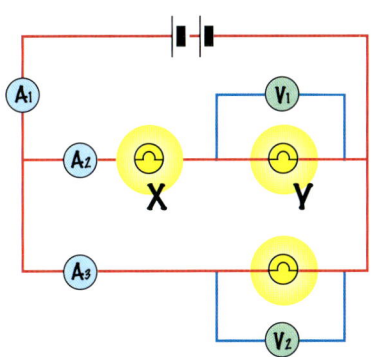

   a) What is the value of the voltage, V_1?

   b) What is the value of the voltage, V_2?

   c) If the reading on the ammeter, A_1 is 6A, what is the reading on (i) ammeter A_2

   (ii) ammeter A_3

   d) If the resistance of each lamp is 20Ω what is the total resistance of lamps X and Y?

3. Car headlamps can be connected in two ways as shown below.

   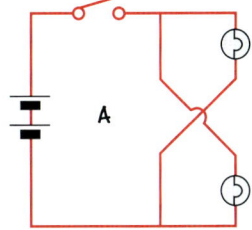   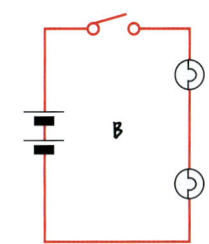

   Which circuit would you recommend?
   Give reasons for your answer.

4. a) For the following parallel circuits state which lamps are on and which lamps are off.

   (i) 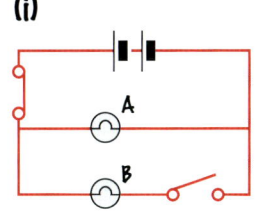   (ii) 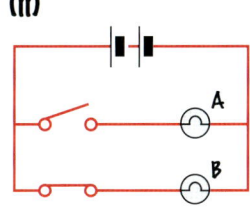   (iii) 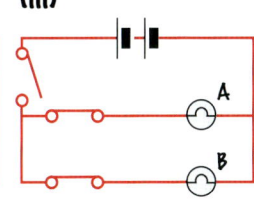   (iv) 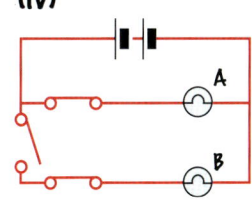   (v)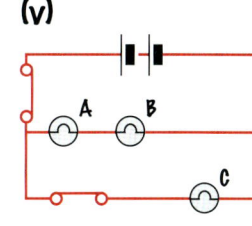

   A is ....   A is ....   A is ....   A is ....   A is ....
   B is ....   B is ....   B is ....   B is ....   B is ....
                                                                                                  C is ....

   b) House lights are connected in parallel. State ONE advantage and ONE disadvantage.

   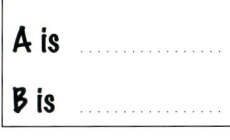

ELECTRICAL POWER

Basic Electricity

1. It is important that electrical appliances are fitted with the correct fuse.
   Complete the table below by calculating:

   a) the normal working current.   b) the correct fuse that should be fitted.

Appliance	Power Rating	P.D. (V)	Working Current (A)	Fuse Size (1A, 3A, 5A, 13A)
Iron	1000	230		
Food Mixer	460	230		
Sewing Machine	800	230		
Hi - Fi	115	230		
Hoover	1500	230		
Computer	100	230		
Electric Fire	2000	230		
Hair Drier	500	230		

2. An electric light bulb has a power rating of 100W. The potential difference across it is 230V.

   What current flows through it?

3. An electric drill works at a current of 5A and a voltage of 230V.

   What is the power rating of the motor inside the drill?

4. UK mains voltage changed recently from 240V to 230V.

   For an appliance with a working current of 8A. Calculate its power rating at:

   a) 240V

   b) 230V

5. The circuit diagram shows a parallel circuit.

   The potential difference across each lamp is 12V. Each lamp has a resistance of 5Ω.

   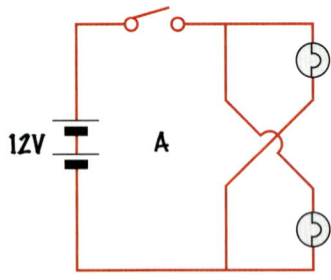

   a) Calculate the current passing through each lamp.

   b) Suggest a suitable fuse for the circuit.

   b) Calculate the total power supplied to the lamps.

PAYING FOR ELECTRICITY

Basic Electricity

1. The table shows the power rating of different electrical appliances and how long they are switched on for each week.

   For each appliance calculate: a) the energy transferred each week in joules
   b) the energy transferred each week in KWh and   c) the cost per week (electricity costs 8p per unit)

Appliance	Power Rating (W)	Time Used Each Week	Energy Transferred (J)	Energy Transferred (kWh)	Cost Per Week (p)
Kettle	1500	6h			
Immersion Heater	3000	5h			
Cooker	4000	15h			
Electric Fire	2000	30h			
Hair Drier	750	3h			
Iron	1000	2h			
Washing Machine	2500	6h 30min			
Tumble Drier	2000	30min			
Electric Shower	8000	3h			

2. The picture shows part of an electricity bill.

   REB Regional **Electricity** Board
   Customer No. 3 263 1319 12
   Statement Date 26 Sept 1999
   Most recent reading 47209.4 kWh
   Previous reading 45959.5 kWh
   Units used _____ kWh (Units)
   units at 6.9p per unit = _____

   a) Calculate the number of units used.

   b) Calculate the cost of the electricity.

3. Fred decided to check his electricity bill since the last two bills had only been estimates. The previous estimated meter reading was 34215. The present meter reading is shown below.

   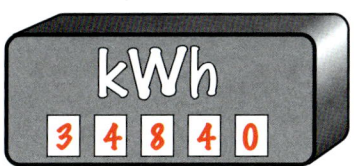

   a) How many units of electricity has Fred used since the estimate?

   b) If electricity costs 8p per unit, how much does Fred owe the electricity company?

4. Sam's mum is always complaining that when he leaves his room at night he always leaves all the electrical appliances on. He decides to work out how much they cost. He writes down their power rating.

   One electric fire 2kW, Three light bulbs each 100W, One CD player 100W.
   He left the appliances on for five hours while he went out.

   a) Calculate the cost of leaving these appliances on. Electricity costs 8p per unit.

   b) What would the cost be over a three month period if he did this every night? (assume three months is 90 days).

ELECTRICITY IN THE HOME

Basic Electricity

1. a) Explain the difference between a.c. and d.c.

   b) What is the frequency of the mains supply in the UK?

2. The diagram below shows different appliances connected to the mains supply. The appliances shown are all on. Each appliance has a voltage of 230V across it.

   Supply = 230V
   30A Fuse
   Toaster 720W
   Washing Machine 1500W
   Tumble Drier 2000W
   Electric Iron 1000W
   Kettle 1200W

   a) Calculate the current flowing through.

   (i) the Toaster .... (ii) the Washing Machine ....

   (iii) the Tumble Dryer .... (iv) the Electric Iron ....

   (v) the Kettle ....

   b) Is the fuse rating big enough to take all of these appliances when they are on. Explain your answer.

HIGHER/SPECIAL TIER

3. The picture shows part of a wiring diagram for a home.

   Ring Main Circuit

   Lighting Circuit

   a) Complete the diagram by
      (i) Drawing a circuit diagram for the ring main circuit which has four sockets in it.
      (ii) Draw a circuit diagram for the lighting circuit which has four light sockets in it.
   b) How many 100W light bulbs could be connected in the lighting circuit shown?
      Show your working (remember each bulb will have a p.d. (voltage) of 230V across it).

   c) What could the circuit labelled A be used for?

THE THREE PIN PLUG — Basic Electricity

1. Complete the diagram of the three pin plug below by

   a) Drawing in the missing parts.

   b) Labelling all the parts.

   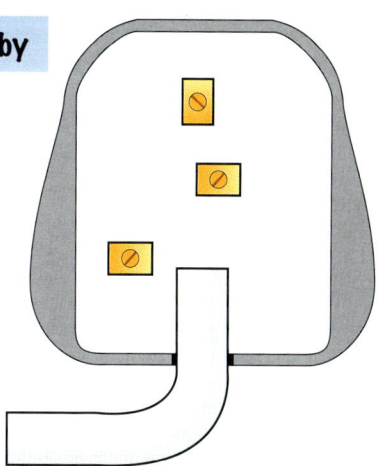

2. For each of the following three pin plugs find three faults for each one

   a) 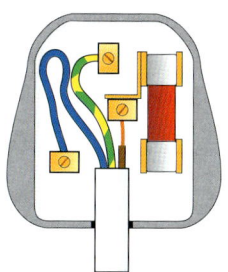   b) 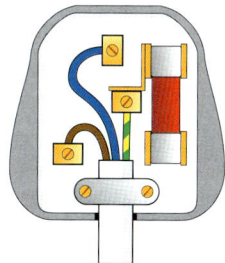   c) 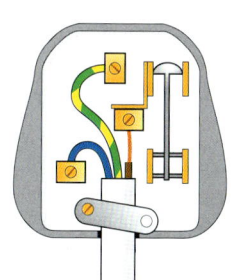   d)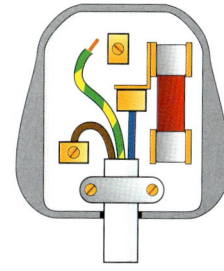

   (i) ....
   (ii) ....
   (iii) ....

   (i) ....
   (ii) ....
   (iii) ....

   (i) ....
   (ii) ....
   (iii) ....

   (i) ....
   (ii) ....
   (iii) ....

3. The different parts of the plug named below are all made from a suitable material. Name a suitable material and give a reason for your choice.

   a) Pins.

   b) Inner core of wire.

   c) Casing of the plug.

   d) Outer core of wire.

G.C.S.E. Ref: Page 36

FUSES AND DOUBLE INSULATION

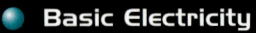

Basic Electricity

1. The diagram shows a hair dryer. The hair dryer has a plastic casing.

   a) The hair dryer plug has only two wires. Which two?

   (i) ....

   (ii) ....

   b) Which of the usual three wires is missing?

   c) The hairdryer is safe to use without the third wire, explain why.

   230V 50Hz
   MAXIMUM POWER 1000W.

   d) The following information is found on the hair dryer.

   (i) Calculate the maximum current the hair dryer should take.

   (ii) Name a suitable size of fuse for the hair dryer.

   e) During use a fault occurs and a current of 30A flows through the live wire.

   (i) Suggest a possible reason for a fault occurring.

   (ii) Describe and explain what happens to the fuse.

   (iii) How does this protect the wiring to the hair dryer?

EARTHING AND CIRCUIT BREAKERS

Basic Electricity

1. Electric fires have metal cases. They have three wires connected in the plug. Two of the wires are the live and the neutral.

    a) What is the third wire called?

    b) To what part of the electric fire should this third wire be connected?

    c) If a fault develops in the electric fire, describe how the user is protected from an electric shock.

2. The diagram shows a circuit breaker

    a) What is the job of a circuit breaker?

    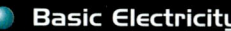

    b) What advantage do circuit breakers have over fuses?

    c) (i) Explain, in detail, what would happen if a surge of current were to flow through the circuit breaker shown.

      (ii) How does this make the circuit safe?

      (iii) Draw a diagram of the circuit breaker after this surge of current.

    d) If the consumer unit of a house still relies on fuses, state a way in which the residents can use a circuit breaker for jobs such as mowing the lawn (with an electric mower).

    e) Why should circuit breakers and fuses always be placed in the live wire circuit?

G.C.S.E. Ref: Page 38 — *Lonsdale* Science Revision Guides - Physics Double Award Higher/Special & Foundation Tiers

MAGNETISM

Electricity and Magnetism

1. The diagram shows a bar magnet which is allowed to swing freely in the Earth's magnetic field.

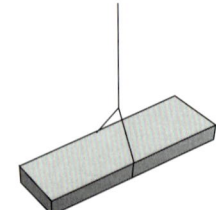

   a) Complete the diagram by including the direction of the north pole of the Earth's magnetic field and labelling the north and south poles on the bar magnet.

   b) Another piece of metal is brought up to the bar magnet. It is attracted. What does this tell you about the metal?

   c) How could you test to see if the metal is a magnet or not? Explain your answer.

   d) Complete the diagrams below by drawing the shapes of the magnetic fields that surround these magnets.

   (i) [N S]   (ii) [S] [S]

   (iii) [N] [S]   (iv) [N] [N]

2. The diagram shows a magnetic switch. It is being used as a burglar alarm in a window.

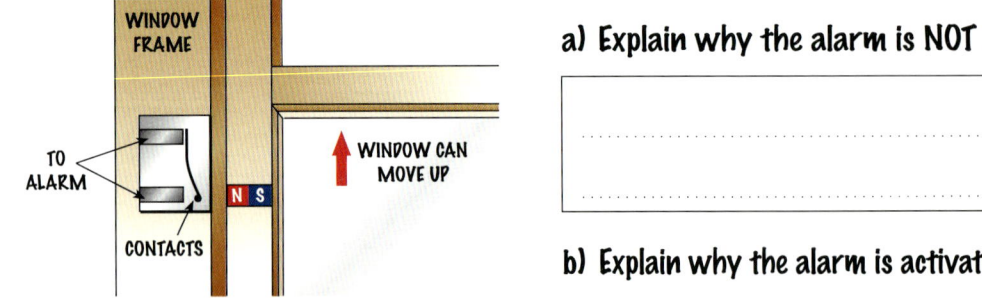

   a) Explain why the alarm is NOT activated.

   b) Explain why the alarm is activated when the window is open.

3. The thickness of paint on cars can be measured by using a magnet attached to a force meter. The diagrams show a very simplified arrangement.

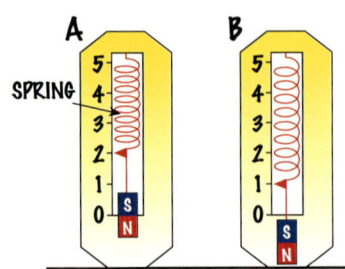

   a) In which diagram is the paint the thickest?

   b) Explain how this paint thickness measurer works.

32   Lonsdale Science Revision Guides - Physics Double Award Higher/Special & Foundation Tiers   G.C.S.E. Ref: Page 41

ELECTROMAGNETISM

Electricity and Magnetism

1. Harry is carrying out an investigation into the factors that affect the strength of an electromagnet. He decides to investigate how the strength depends on the number of turns of wire on the coil.

    a) State two other factors that will affect the strength of the electromagnet.

    (i) ....   (ii) ....

    b) Harry decided he would see how many paper clips the electromagnet could pick up. How will he carry out a fair test?

    c) The results of Harry's experiment are shown below.

    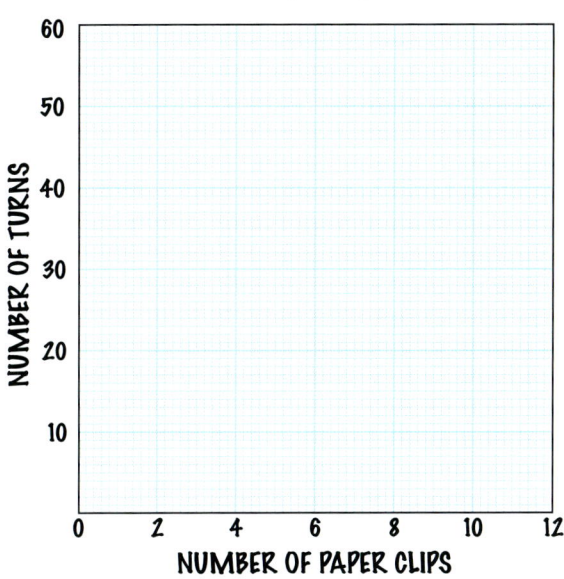

Number of turns	0	10	20	30	40	50	60
Number of paper clips	0	2	4		8	11	12

    (i) Plot a graph of his results and use it to find the missing result in the table above.

    (ii) What conclusion can Harry come to from these results?

2. Steel is used to make permanent magnets.

    a) Describe with the aid of a diagram, how this can be done.

    b) Why is steel and not soft iron used to make permanent magnets?

APPLICATIONS OF ELECTROMAGNETISM

Electricity and Magnetism

1. The diagram shows a 'ding-dong' door bell. The bell works by hitting the chimes labelled A and B.

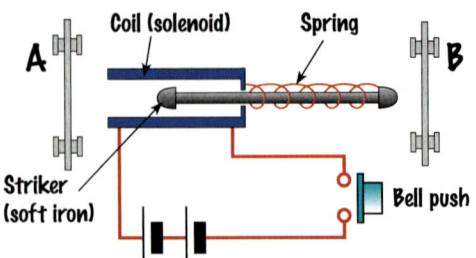

a) What happens to the solenoid when the bell push is pressed?

b) Why is the striker made of soft iron?

c) What happens to the soft iron striker when the bell push is pressed?

d) What is the purpose of the spring?

e) Describe how the 'ding-dong' door bell works.

f) The manufacture has received complaints that the bell is not loud enough. Suggest two ways they could change this design to make the bell louder? Explain your answers.

A
B

2. The diagram opposite shows a simple arrangement for a burglar alarm. A door has been opened and the alarm has been activated.

a) What is the name of this particular device?

b) Explain fully what happens to the alarm when the door is closed.

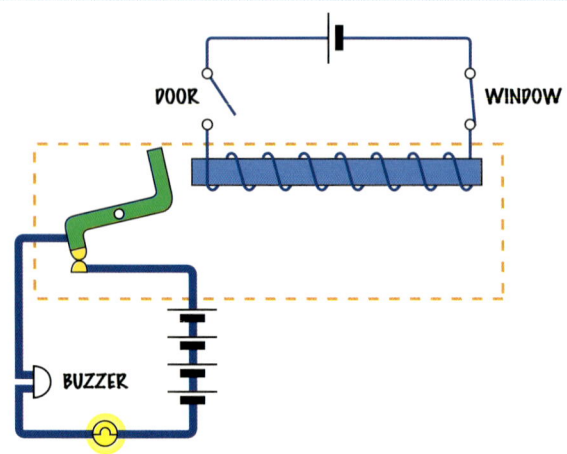

c) Draw a diagram to show the alarm after the door has been closed.

34 — Lonsdale Science Revision Guides - Physics Double Award Higher/Special & Foundation Tiers — G.C.S.E. Ref: Page 43

THE MOTOR EFFECT

Electricity and Magnetism

1. The diagram shows a 'kicking wire' experiment used to demonstrate the motor effect.

   a) When the switch is closed the wire moves as shown.
      Explain why the wire moves.

   b) State two ways in which the wire could be made to move in the other direction.
      (i) ....
      (ii) ....

   c) The apparatus is rearranged. Describe the change in the movement of the wire if:
      (i) Four cells are used instead of two.

      (ii) A weaker magnet is used.

   d) Explain what would happen to the wire if an a.c. supply was used instead of the d.c. supply shown.

2. The moving coil loudspeaker is a device that uses the principles of the motor effect. The following statements describe how a moving coil loudspeaker works. They are not in the correct order.

   A ... creating a FORCE which causes the cardboard cone to move in one direction ...

   B ... when the current flows through the coil in ONE DIRECTION this creates a MAGNETIC FIELD ...

   C ... creating SOUND WAVES ...

   D ... since the current is alternating this will cause the cone to vibrate back and forth ...

   E ... which INTERACTS with the PERMANENT MAGNETIC FIELD ...

   F ... when the current CHANGES DIRECTION ...

   G ... the cone moves in the opposite direction ...

   a) Put the statements in the correct order by writing the letters in the boxes below.

   □ → □ → □ → □ → □ → □ → □

   b) Why does the loudspeaker use a 'varying alternating current'?

   c) What happens to the current when the sound gets louder (bigger vibrations)?

G.C.S.E. Ref: Page 44 — Lonsdale Science Revision Guides - Physics Double Award Higher/Special & Foundation Tiers

THE DIRECT CURRENT MOTOR

Electricity and Magnetism

1. The diagram show a simple direct current motor. The following statements describe how the motor works.

   A ... which interacts with the magnetic field of the magnet ...
   B ... so the coil rotates ...
   C ... as a current flows through the coil ...
   D ... creating a force on both sides of the coil ...
   E ... this creates a magnetic field ...

   a) Place the statements in the correct order. ☐ → ☐ → ☐ → ☐ → ☐

   b) For each of the following statements state what effect they will have on the speed of rotation of the motor.

   (i) The strength of the magnetic field is decreased.

   (ii) A soft iron core is placed inside the coil.

   (iii) The number of turns on the coil is increased.

   (iv) The size of the current through the coil is decreased.

HIGHER/SPECIAL TIER

2. For the electric motors shown below use Fleming's left hand rule to work out the direction of rotation of the motor.

   a)   b)   c)   d)

3. The following motors all rotate. Complete each diagram by either labelling the direction of flow of current through the coil or the polarity of the magnets.

   a)   b)   c)   d)

4. The diagram shows an electric motor.

   a) Describe in detail how the motor works, paying particular attention to the job of the split ring commutator.

ELECTROMAGNETIC INDUCTION

Electricity and Magnetism

1. The diagrams below show a wire and a magnet.

   For each combination of wire and magnet draw the meter reading you would expect to see.
   The first one has been done for you.

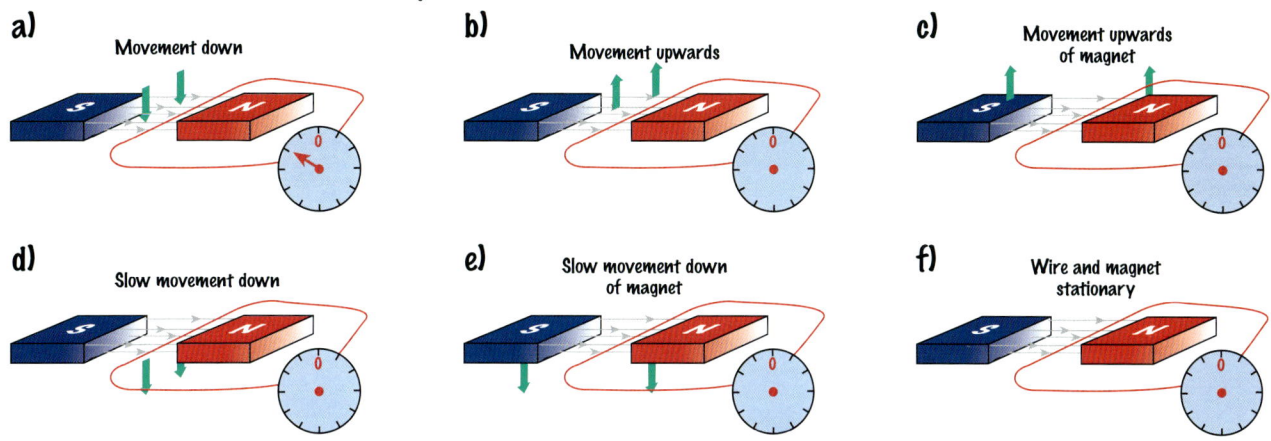

   a) Movement down

   b) Movement upwards

   c) Movement upwards of magnet

   d) Slow movement down

   e) Slow movement down of magnet

   f) Wire and magnet stationary

2. The diagram below shows a bar magnet moving towards a coil of wire. The meter shows a reading.

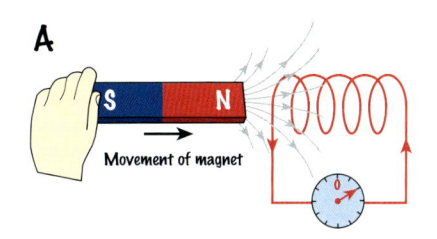

   A

   a) For the diagrams shown below describe the motion of the magnet compared to diagram A. You should use the following words: 'same speed', 'faster', 'slower', 'same direction', 'opposite direction', 'no movement'.

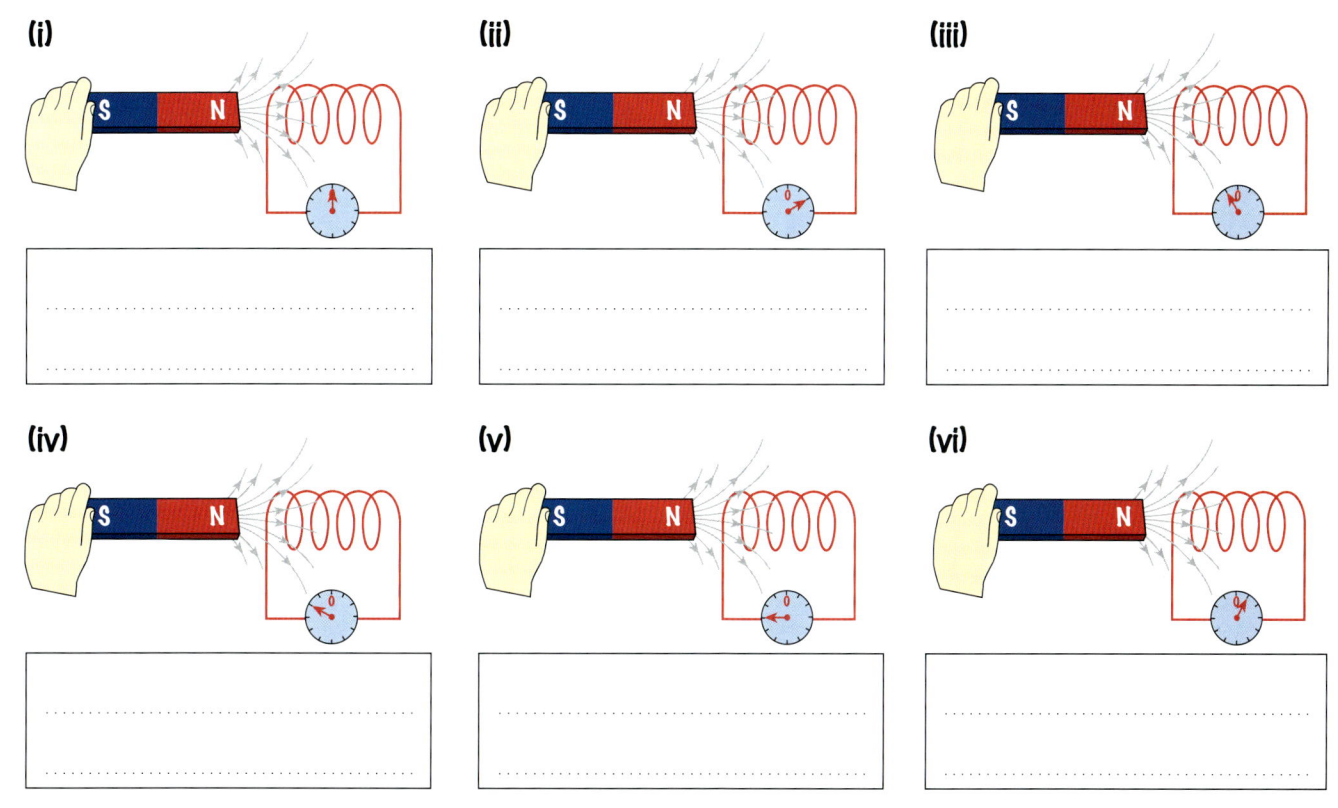

   (i)

   (ii)

   (iii)

   (iv)

   (v)

   (vi)

   b) Apart from altering the speed of movement of the magnet state two ways of altering the induced voltage.

   (i) ....

   (ii) ....

G.C.S.E. Ref: Page 46 — *Lonsdale* Science Revision Guides - Physics Double Award Higher/Special & Foundation Tiers — 37

APPLICATIONS OF ELECTROMAGNETIC INDUCTION — Electricity and Magnetism

HIGHER/SPECIAL TIER

1. The diagram shows a generator.

   a) The current output from the generator was measured every 0.1s for 1.2s.
   The results are shown in the table.

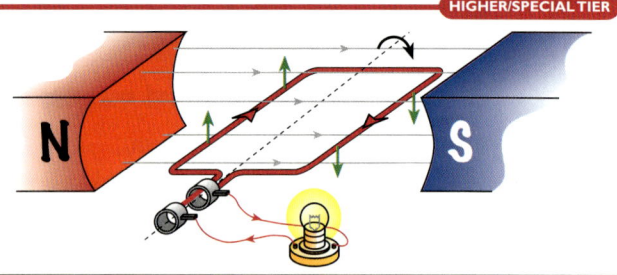

Time (s)	0	0.1	0.2	0.3	0.4	0.5	0.6	0.7	0.8	0.9	1.0	1.1	1.2
Current Output (A)	0	1.5	2.6	3	2.6	1.5	0	-1.5	-2.6	-3	-2.6	-1.5	0

   Draw a graph of current against time on the axes opposite.

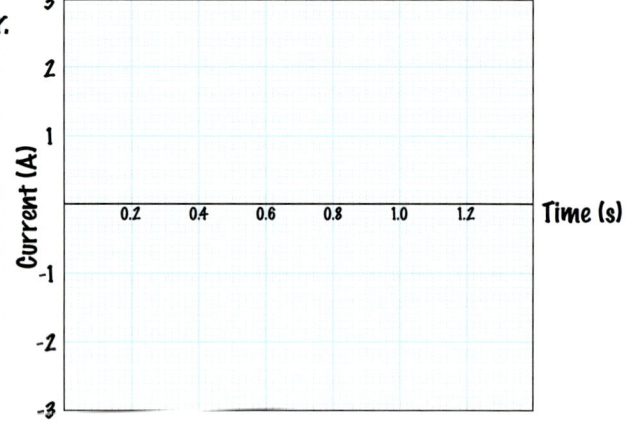

   i) Is the current output a.c. or d.c.? Explain your answer.

   b) What is the purpose of the slip rings and brush contacts?

   c) Explain, in as much detail as possible how the generator produces electricity.

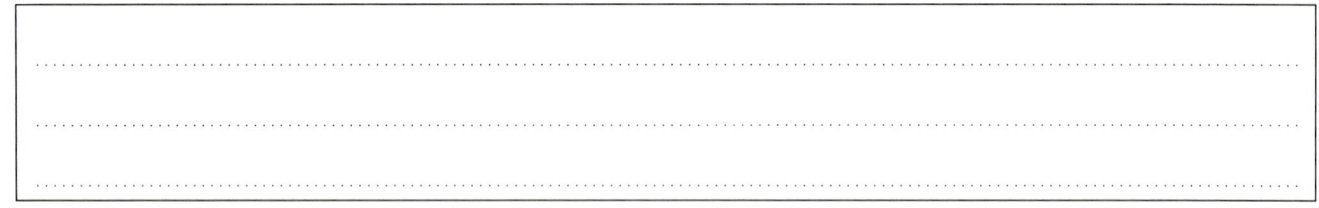

   d) The current output from a different generator is shown below. On the same axes sketch graphs to show the output when:

   (i) The coil of wire is rotating at the same rate (speed) but the strength of the magnetic field is increased. Label this graph (i)

   (ii) The coil of wire is rotated twice as quickly. Label this graph (ii)

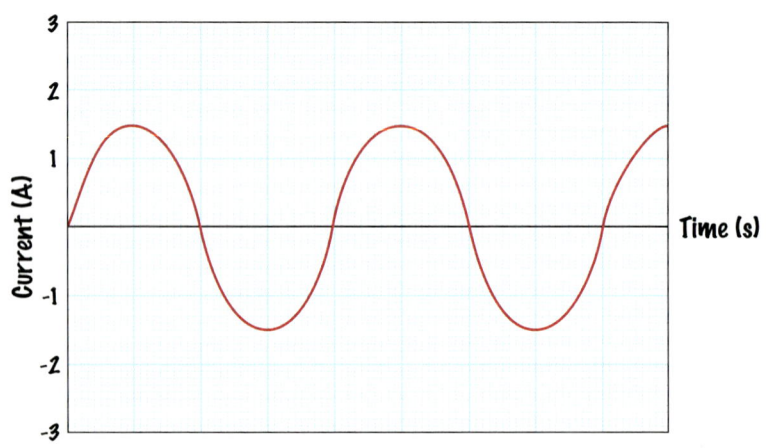

2. The moving coil microphone and tape playback are both applications of electromagnetic induction.

   a) Name one other way that they are both similar to each other in the way they work.

   b) Name one way that they are different to each other in the way they work.

TRANSMISSION OF ELECTRICITY

Electricity and Magnetism

1. The diagram below shows how electricity is distributed from power stations to shops, factories and houses all over the country.

   a) What is the name given to this electrical distribution network?

   b) What are transformers A and B used for?

   c) What type of transformer would you find at:

   (i) A .... (ii) B ....

2. A generator at a power station produces 500 MW of electrical energy. The table below gives the possible voltage and current values that the electricity can be transmitted at.

Voltage (KV)	Current (A)
100	5000
150	3300
200	2500
250	2000
300	1700
350	1400
400	1300

   a) Draw a graph of voltage against current.

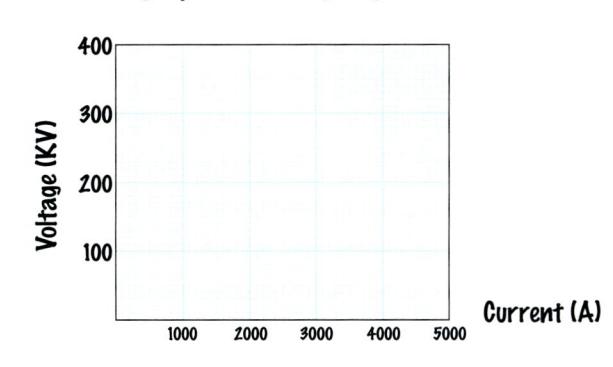

   b) (i) If the electricity is transmitted at a voltage of 275KV, what current flows through the power lines.

   (ii) If the current flowing through the power lines is 3000A at what voltage is the electricity transmitted at?

   c) Explain why the electricity is transmitted at a high voltage and a low current.

   d) The thickness of the cable that the electricity is transmitted through is also an important consideration. Explain why there is a compromise thickness.

TRANSFORMERS

Electricity and Magnetism

HIGHER/SPECIAL TIER

1. The diagram shows a transformer.

   a) Name the material used to make the core of the transformer.

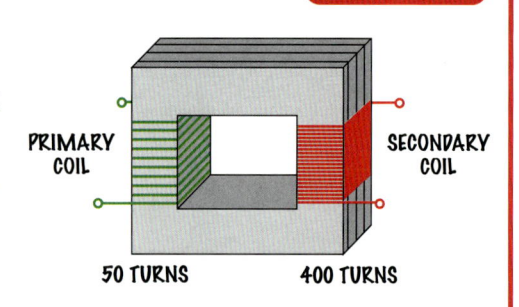

   PRIMARY COIL — 50 TURNS
   SECONDARY COIL — 400 TURNS

   b) Explain, in detail, how the transformer works.

   c) If the voltage applied to the primary coil is 12V. Calculate the voltage across the secondary coil.

2. For each transformer calculate:

   a) The number of turns on secondary coil.

   1000 TURNS, Vp = 230V, Vs = 230,000V

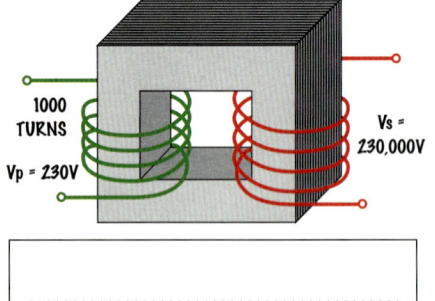

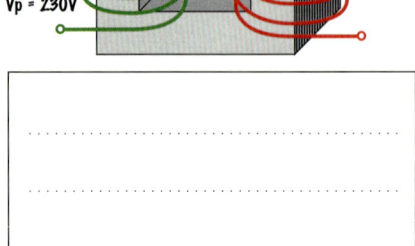

   b) The voltage across the primary coil.

   18,000 TURNS, 100 TURNS, Vs = 230V

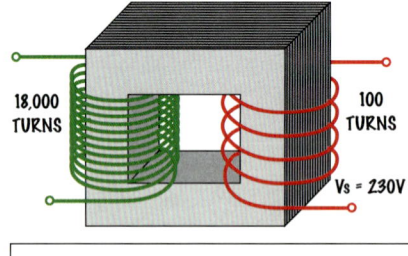

   c) The voltage across the secondary coil.

   1000 TURNS, 12V d.c., 1200 TURNS

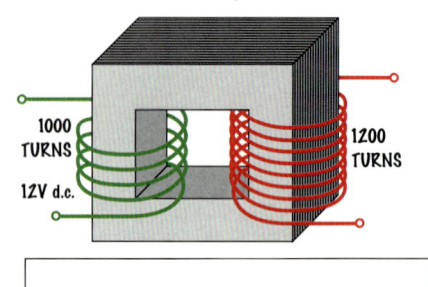

3. Transformer has 1000 turns on its primary coil and 100 turns on its secondary coil. The voltage across the primary is 230 volts.

   a) Calculate the voltage across the secondary.

   b) If the current in the primary coil is 2A and the current in the secondary coil is 18A. Calculate:

   (i) the power input

   (ii) the power output

   (iii) The efficiency of the transformer.

   c) Explain how laminating the core makes the transformer more efficient.

CONDUCTION OF HEAT

Energy

1. The diagram shows a typical experiment carried out in the school laboratory to illustrate the conduction of heat.

   hot water, glass rod, drawing pins held on with vaseline, copper rod

   a) Which drawing pin would you expect to drop off first? Explain your answer.

   b) Explain how heat is conducted through solids.

2. The drawing shows 2 kettles.

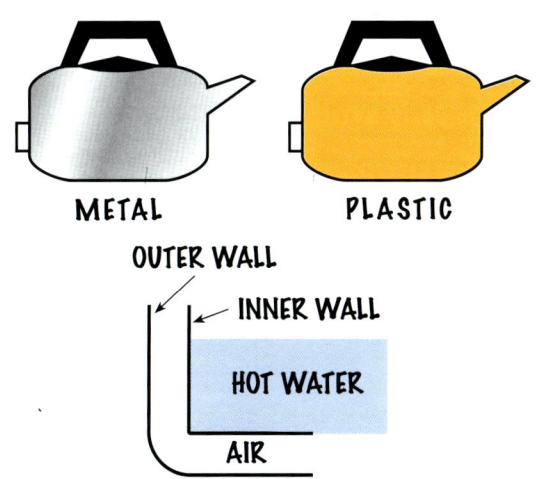

   METAL — PLASTIC
   OUTER WALL, INNER WALL, HOT WATER, AIR

   a) If the same amount of water was boiled in each kettle and then left to cool which kettle would you expect to stay hottest the longest. Explain your answer.

   b) Some kettles have double walls. Suggest, with reasons, one advantage of having a double-walled kettle.

3. One way of reducing heat loss from hot water cylinders is to lag the tank. Explain how lagging reduces heat loss from the tank.

4. Explain the following:

   a) Fleeces keep us warm.

   b) Newspaper can keep ice cream cold and fish and chips hot.

   c) Cool boxes are lined with expanded polystyrene (polystyrene with air bubbles in).

   d) Quilts keep us warm at night.

CONVECTION OF HEAT

● Energy

1. When an electric kettle is switched on it will take a few minutes to boil the water.

   a) Explain, in detail, how the kettle element heats all the water.

2. The diagram shows a coal fire.

   a) Explain why a lot of the heat from the fire is lost up the chimney.

   b) Explain how the coal fire helps to ventilate the room.

3. a) Explain why ocean currents move from equatorial regions towards the polar regions.

   b) What would happen if all of the Earth received the same amount of heat from the Sun?

4. Describe, with the aid of diagrams, why we get land and sea breezes.

Land Breezes	Sea Breezes

5. Explain the following:

   a) The cooler compartment is at the top of a fridge.

   b) An ice-cube cools all of the drink.

RADIATION AND EVAPORATION OF HEAT — Energy

1. Explain the following:

a) A car radiator is dull black.

b) It is an advantage for polar bears to have white fur (not just for camouflage).

c) A solar panel works by heating up water in pipes. Explain why:
   (i) The pipes are dull black.

   (ii) the back of the panel is shiny.

d) In some countries plasterboard has one side that is "silvered" these are often used for ceilings, especially in the roof. Why does this help:
   (i) to keep the house cool in the summer.

   (ii) to keep the house warm in winter.

e) The silvering on a vacuum flask helps to keep hot tea hot and cold drinks cold. Explain why this is so.

2. Carbon dioxide is called a 'greenhouse gas' and contributes to 'global warming'. Explain why this is so.

3. Alison and Hugh were swimming at the local outdoor pool. Alison had been in the water and Hugh had not.

a) Explain why Alison felt cold when she came out of the water and stood around.

b) Suddenly a gust of wind blew. Alison felt even colder. Explain why

ENERGY TRANSFER IN ACTION

● Energy

1. The diagram shows a house. The house has not been insulated.

   The table shows how some parts of the house may be insulated to reduce energy losses. The cost of each method is also given.

Where the Energy is lost	Method of insulation	Cost of insulation (£)	Annual Saving	Pay Back Time
roof		300	75	
walls		800	40	
windows		3000	100	
doors		20	20	

   a) Complete the table.

   b) Which method of insulation would you install first? Explain why.

   c) (i) Which method of insulation would you install last? Explain why.

   (ii) What are the advantages of installing this method of insulation?

   HIGHER/SPECIAL TIER

2. The U-value for a double glazed window is 3W/m² °C. If a house has 4 windows of this type each of an area of 3m². Calculate the heat energy lost each second when the temperature outside is 5°C and the temperature inside is 20°C.

3. In an industrial process water is heated up from a temperature of 25°C to 90°C.

   a) How much energy is used to heat 2000kg of water? (Specific heat capacity of water is 4200 J/kg°C)

   b) In reality more heat energy than this is needed because the container has to be heated as well. If the container is made of aluminium calculate the total amount of heat energy that is needed. The container has a mass of 400Kg. (Specific heat capacity of aluminium = 800J/kg°C)

ENERGY AND EFFICIENCY

1. For the following electrical devices write down the energy transfer taking place. State which of the energy transfers are wanted and which of the energy transfers are unwanted.

   a) TV set

   b) Hair-dryer

   c) CD player

   d) Toaster

   e) Microwave

   f) TV remote control

   g) Tumble dryer

2. The diagram shows a 100W electric light bulb.

   a) How much energy is given out by the bulb each second?

   b) Some of the energy given out is wasted. Why is some of the energy wasted?

3. The diagram shows a car. For each 100J of energy input into the car 80J is wasted.

   a) What form(s) does the wasted energy take?

   b) What form does the useful energy take?

   c) What is the percentage efficiency of the car?

4. The energy input into a coal fired power station every second is 10,000,000 J. The power station is 35% efficient. Calculate:

   a) The energy output every second.

   b) The energy wasted every second.

NON-RENEWABLE ENERGY RESOURCES — Energy

1. Coal, oil and gas are called fossil fuels, uranium is called a nuclear fuel. Uranium is not really a fuel. Explain why.

2. The picture shows a coal fired power station. Describe how the energy in coal is transferred to drive generators in coal-fired power stations.

3. The energy transfer diagram shows what happens to every 100 joules of energy from the gas burned in a power station.

   .... J

   100J INPUT .... J

   a) Complete the diagram (use your ruler for accuracy).

   b) What form does the wasted energy take?

   c) What happens to the wasted energy?

   d) What is the efficiency of this power station?

4. The data below is for a typical power station.

   Output power 500,000KW
   Energy content of coal 2,700 KJ/Kg
   Total quantity of coal used per day 64,000,000kg
   Use the data to calculate:

   a) The total energy output each day.

   b) The total energy input from the coal each day.

   c) The efficiency of the power station.

RENEWABLE ENERGY RESOURCES   • Energy

1. The diagram shows a method of generating electricity.

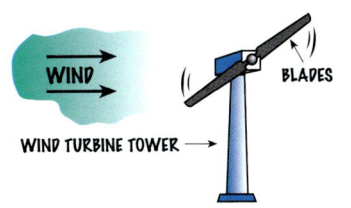

   a) What type of energy does the wind possess to turn the turbine? ....

   b) What is the source of this energy? ....

   c) What is the advantage of generating electricity this way compared to a fossil fuel power station?
   ....

2. The diagram shows a "salter duck" used for generating electricity. Describe how electricity is generated using this method.
   ....
   ....

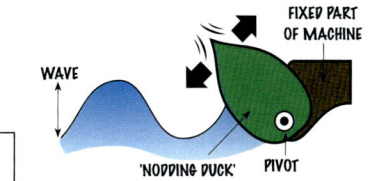

3. Why can burning wood be described as a renewable energy resource?
   ....
   ....

4. Solar cells can be used to generate electricity. Why can they not be used to provide energy for shops and factories?
   ....
   ....

5. Describe how energy from hot rocks under the Earth's surface can be used to generate electricity.
   ....
   ....

6. The diagram shows how tides are used to generate electricity.

   a) Draw an arrow to show the way the water flows through the turbine.

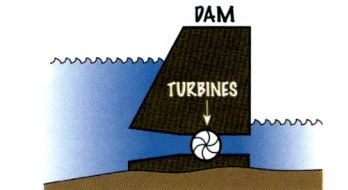

   b) What form of energy is lost by the water as it falls? ....

   c) What form of energy does the water have as it flows through the turbine?
   ....

   d) Tides are a renewable energy resource. Explain what is meant by a renewable energy resource.
   ....

   e) Describe how this method of driving turbines to generate electricity is different from using fossil fuels.
   ....

G.C.S.E. Ref: Page 58

ANALYSIS OF NON-RENEWABLE AND RENEWABLE ENERGY RESOURCES — Energy

1. A power station is to be built to supply electrical energy to the town of Leighshack. The choice is between a coal fired power station, a gas fired power station and a nuclear power station.

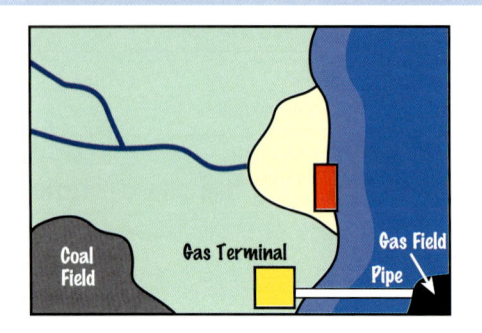

   a) Give ONE advantage and ONE disadvantage for having each type of power station.

   b) Which option would you support? Justify your choice.

2. St George II is a beautiful remote island in the Caribbean. There are no fossil fuel resources on the island. The diagram shows a map of the island. The table below shows the wind speeds and the percentage of time that the wind is at that value. No electricity is generated by wind turbines at a wind speed below 4m/s or above 10m/s.

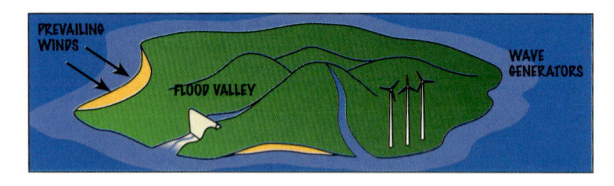

% of time	10	20	30	20	10	5	5
Wind speed (m/s)	2	4	6	8	10	12	14

   a) For what percentage of the time could wind turbines be used to generate electricity?

   b) Discuss the advantages and disadvantages of using wind turbines.

   c) Some islanders suggest that since there are many fast running streams on the island, that hydro-electric power would be a better option. The data shows a rainfall chart for the island.

Rainfall (mm)	20	40	80	120	10	0	0	0	10	10	20	20
Month	J	F	M	A	M	J	J	A	S	O	N	D

   (i) Discuss the advantages and disadvantages of HEP on the island of St George II (remember to use the information)

WORK AND POWER

Energy

1. A cyclist moves along a flat road against a resistive force of 100N. If the cyclist travels 1000m calculate the work done by the cyclist.

2. Donna lifts a parcel of weight 100N onto a shelf that is 2m above the ground.

    a) Calculate the work done in lifting the parcel onto the shelf.

    b) What type of energy does the parcel gain?

3. A car is driven up a mountain pass. It gains a vertical height of 300m. The weight of the car and its passengers is 10,000N.

    a) Calculate the work done by the car against gravity.

    b) What is the gain in potential energy of the car?

4. Matt cycles a distance of 2000m against a resistance force of 150N. He travels this distance in 400s.

    a) Calculate the work done by Matt.

    b) What is Matt's power output?

5. The diagram shows a pumped storage system used to store water in a dam.

    a) Calculate the work done in pumping 10,000N of water from the lower to the upper reservoir.

    b) If it takes 10s to move 10,000N of water from the top to the bottom calculate the power output of the pump.

6. The output power of a crane is 1.6kW. Calculate how long it will take to lift a load of 5,000N through a distance of 8m.

KINETIC ENERGY

Energy

1. a) What is kinetic energy?

   b) A truck of mass 2000kg and a car of mass 1000kg are travelling down a motorway at the same speed:

      (i) Which one has the greatest kinetic energy?

      (ii) Explain your answer.

   c) Two cars of the same mass are travelling down a road. Explain how one car could have more kinetic energy than the other.

2. For the following pairs of objects state which has the most kinetic energy.

   a) A car of mass 1000kg or a lorry of mass 3200kg, both moving at 10m/s.

   b) A car of mass 1000kg moving at 10m/s or a car of mass 1000kg moving at 20m/s.

HIGHER/SPECIAL TIER

3. A car of mass 1000kg moves along a road at a constant speed of 20m/s. Calculate it's kinetic energy.

4. A truck of mass 32,000kg moves along a road with a speed of 10m/s. Calculate the kinetic energy of the truck.

5. A skier of mass 90kg is skiing down a hill at a speed of 15m/s. What is the kinetic energy of the skier?

6. The kinetic energy of a cyclist moving along a road is 5000J. If the mass of the cyclist is 100kg calculate the speed of the cyclist.

7. A motorcyclist and motorcycle have a combined mass of 900kg. If they have 140,000J of kinetic energy calculate their speed.

GRAVITATIONAL POTENTIAL ENERGY — Energy

1. The diagram shows a bungee jumper, at various stages.

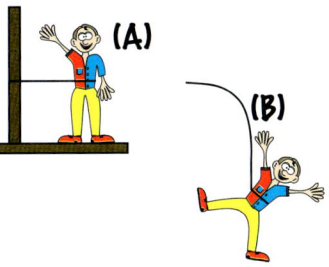

   a) Which type of energy does the jumper have at the top of the jump, (diagram (A))

   b) Which types of energy does the jumper have when falling down? (diagram (B))

   c) If two people, John of mass 60kg and Jill of mass 80kg, were doing the jump, which would have the most energy at the top?

   d) (i) Calculate John's weight.

   (ii) Calculate Jill's weight.

HIGHER/SPECIAL TIER

2. The diagram shows a diver. The mass of the diver is 70kg. The gravitational field strength is 10N/Kg.

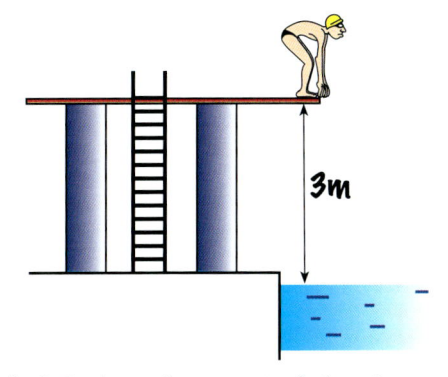

   a) Calculate the weight of the diver?

   b) Calculate the gain in gravitational potential energy as the diver climbs from the pool to the diving board.

   c) Calculate the speed of the diver on entry to the pool.

3. The diagram shows a hydro-electric power plant.

   a) The upper reservoir is 200m above the turbine. The upper reservoir contains 10 million tonnes of water. What is the total potential energy contained in the upper reservoir compared to the turbine?

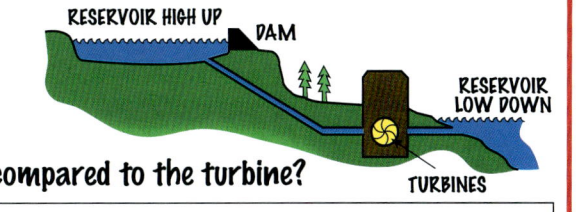

   b) In one second 10,000kg of water flows down the pipe. What is the potential energy of 10,000kg of water in the upper reservoir?

   c) What would be the speed of this 10,000kg of water when it reaches the turbine?

CHARACTERISTICS OF WAVES

1. a) What is a wave? Name the two types of wave.

b) What is the difference between the two types of wave?

2. The diagram shows a waterwave. Eight of the waves are produced every 4 seconds.

(i) Calculate the wavelength of the wave.

(ii) Calculate the frequency of the wave.

(iii) What is the amplitude of the wave?

(iv) Name the points labelled A and B.

A:

B:

3. The diagram shows a wave.

a) What type of wave is shown in the diagram?

b) Draw on the diagram
(i) the direction the wave is moving
(ii) the vibration of one particle of the wave.

(c) Measure the wavelength of this wave?

(d) If the source of the wave is vibrating backwards and forwards 120 times every minute what is the frequency of the wave?

(e) Give an example of this type of wave.

4. The picture shows Toni making waves with a rope.

a) What type of wave is travelling along the rope?

b) The frequency of the wave is 2 hertz. What does this mean?

c) The amplitude of the wave is 75cm and its wavelength is 2m. Label these two distances on the diagram

REFLECTION, REFRACTION AND THE WAVE EQUATION • Waves

1. The diagram shows a ripple tank. In the ripple tank is a barrier.
   Complete the diagram to show the reflection of the waves by the barrier.

   WATER WAVES   RIPPLE TANK

2. The diagram shows water waves going from deep water to shallow water.
   a) Continue the path of the water waves as they go into the shallow water.
   b) What is this effect called?
   c) Continue the path of the water waves as they leave the shallow water and go back into deep water.
   d) Explain why the water waves behave in this way.

HIGHER/SPECIAL TIER

3. A wave has a frequency of 300Hz and a wavelength of 10m. Calculate the speed of the wave.

4. A radio station transmits at a wavelength of 252m. The speed of radio waves is 300000000m/s. Calculate the frequency of these radio waves.

5. An ultrasonic sound wave has a frequency of 25000Hz. The speed of sound in air is 340m/s and in water is 1500 m/s. Calculate the wavelength of the sound in
   a) air
   b) water

6. The Bay Radio Station transmit on a frequency of 96.9 MHz.
   a) What does a frequency of 96.9 MHz mean?
   b) The speed of radio waves is 300 million m/s. Calculate the wavelength of these waves.

DIFFRACTION

Waves

HIGHER/SPECIAL TIER

1. Complete the following diagrams.

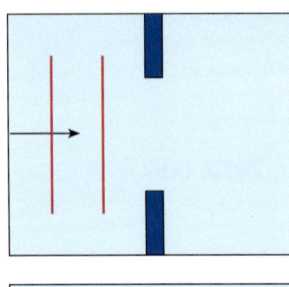

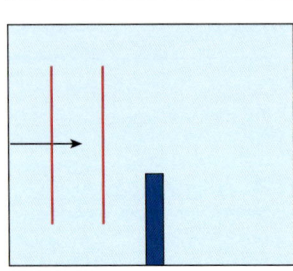

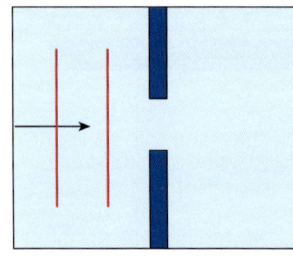

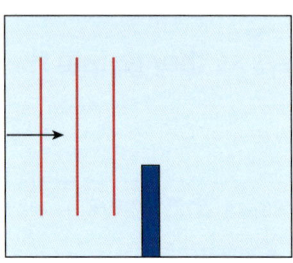

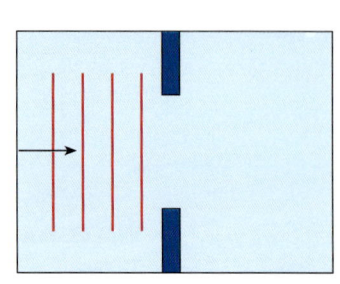

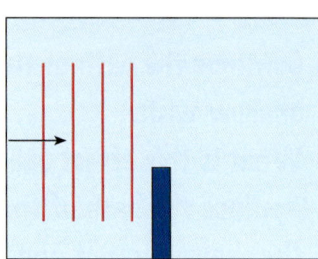

2. All electromagnetic waves travel at a speed of 300 million m/s in air

   a) Calculate the wavelength of a radio station that broadcasts at a frequency of 900 KHz.

   b) Calculate the wavelength of a TV station that broadcasts at a frequency of 500 000 KHz.

   c) (i) Complete the diagram to show what happens to the radio waves in part a) as they pass a hill.

   RADIO AND TV WAVES FROM TRANSMITTER

   (ii) What is the name given to the process which changes the shape of the waves?

   (iii) Explain why the people in the house would be unlikely to receive the television signal's broadcast from the TV station in b) even though they have the correct aerial.

3. Explain why sounds spread out through doorways into regions where you would not expect to hear them.

REFLECTION AND REFRACTION OF LIGHT — Waves

1. The diagram shows a periscope in use. The periscope consists of two mirrors. Draw accurately the path of a ray of light through the periscope.

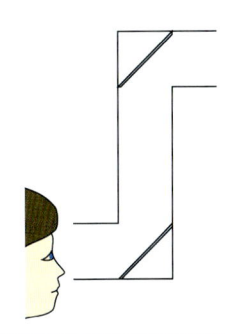

   light from the golfers head

2. The diagram shows three rays of light striking a perspex block.

   a) Complete the paths of the rays through the block and out into the air again.

   b) Explain why the rays have behaved in the way that you have drawn.

3. An experiment was carried out where the passage of a ray of light through a semi-circular glass block was drawn at different angles of incidence. The angle of refraction and reflection were measured for each ray of light. The results are as follows:

Ray	Angle of Incidence	Angle of Refraction	Angle of Reflection
1	10°	15°	10°
2	20°	31°	19°
3	30°	49°	31°
4	40°	75°	40°
5	50°		51°
6	60°		60°
7	70°		70°
8	80°		81°

   a) Complete the diagram opposite. Ray 1 has been drawn for you.

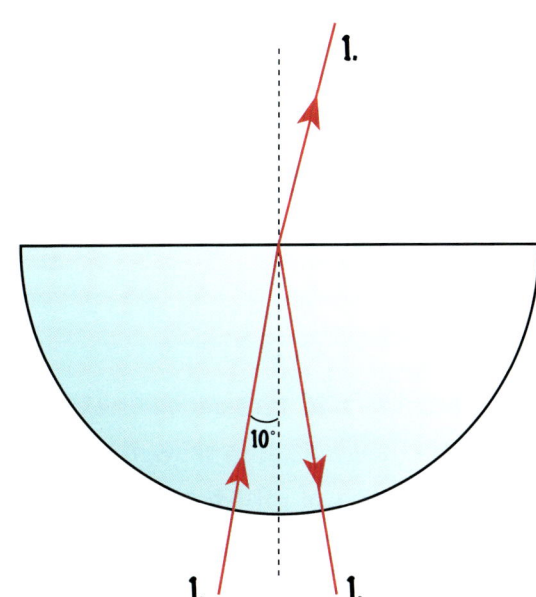

   b) Explain why rays 5 to 8 are not refracted but only reflected.

G.C.S.E. Ref: Page 68

USES OF TOTAL INTERNAL REFLECTION — Waves

1. The diagram shows a length of optical fibre. The critical angle for this fibre is 42°

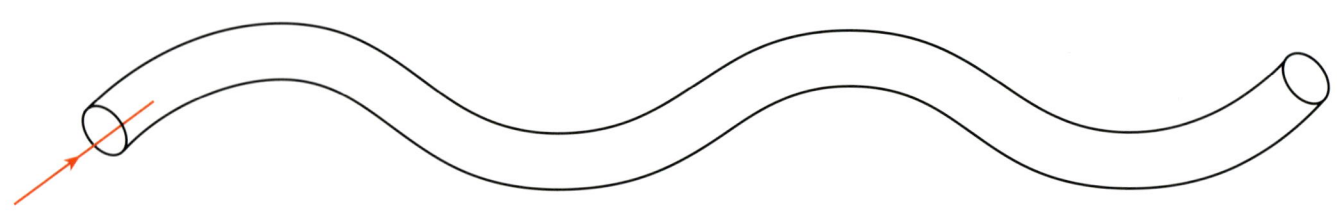

   a) Complete accurately the passage of the ray of light through the fibre. Make sure you mark in all the angles of incidence and reflection.

   b) Fibre optics cable are used for telecommunications. Explain its advantages over electrical signals.

2. An endoscope is a type of instrument that can be used by a doctor to see inside a patients knee. The instrument uses optical fibres.

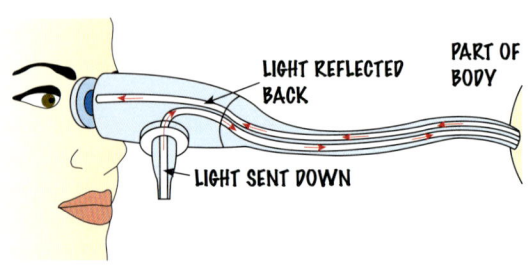

   LIGHT REFLECTED BACK — PART OF BODY — LIGHT SENT DOWN

   Explain, using the diagram to help you if you wish, how the endoscope works.

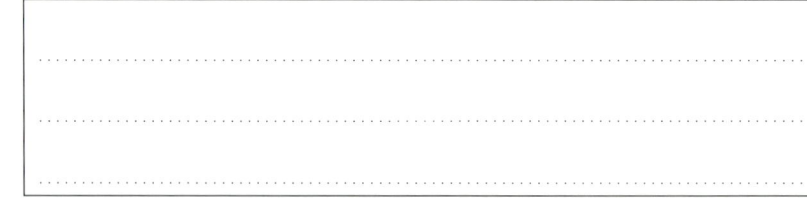

3. a) Reflecting prisms are used in periscopes. Complete the diagram to show

   (i) the arrangement of the prisms and
   (ii) the path of a ray of light through the periscope.
   (iii) What advantage is there in having this type of periscope compared to a mirror periscope.

   b) (i) They are also used in prism binoculars. Complete the diagram to show the passage of the two rays of light through the binoculars.

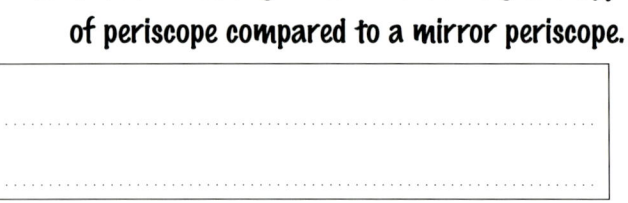

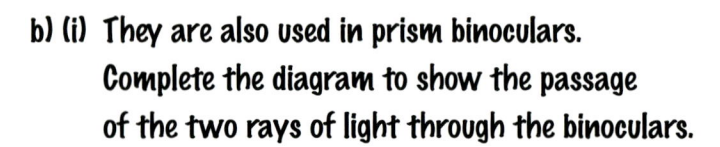

   (ii) What advantage is there in having these prisms inside the binoculars.

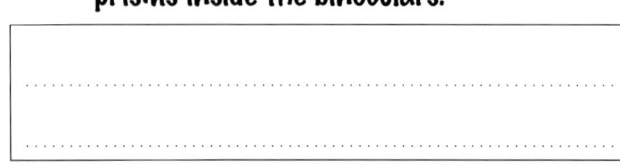

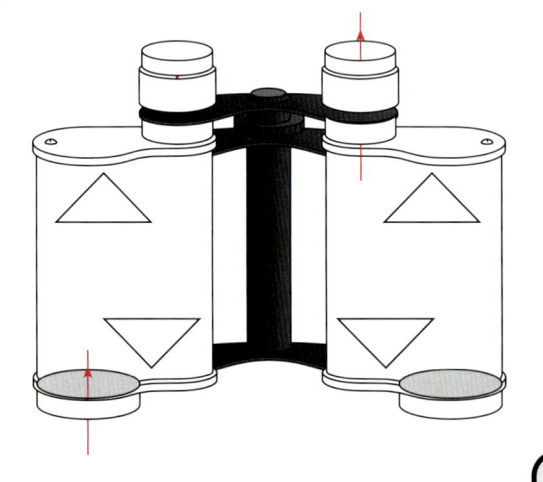

OPTICAL DEVICES — Waves

1. a) Name three different types of mirror

(I) .... (II) .... (III) ....

b) For each of the diagrams below complete the reflection of the rays from the mirrors.

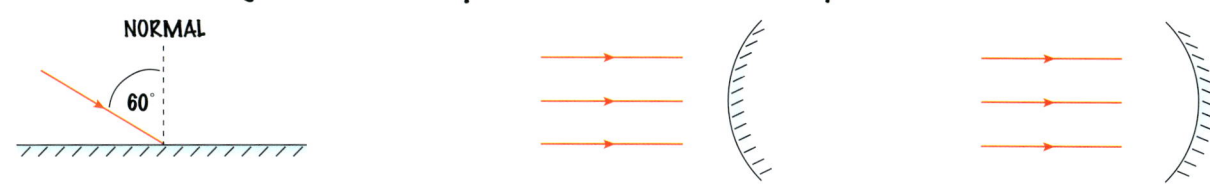

c) For each of the following applications complete the table by writing down the nature of the image required and the type of mirror used.

Application	Nature of image	Type of mirror
Shaving mirror		
Car driving mirror		
Car wing mirror		
Staircase mirror on a bus		
Make-up mirror		
Shop security mirror		

2. The diagram shows two lenses

a) Complete the path of the rays of light through the two lenses

b) Describe the change in the path of the rays that you would expect to see if the lenses were thinner.

....

c) Convex lenses can be used in many optical devices such as a camera, the eye and a slide projector.
For each of these devices state
(i) the nature of the image formed
(ii) the distance from the object to the lens compared to the distance from the image to the lens.

A the camera ....

B the eye ....

C the projector ....

ELECTROMAGNETIC SPECTRUM — Waves

1. **The drawing below shows a triangular prism**

   a) Complete the path of the white light and the red light through the prism.

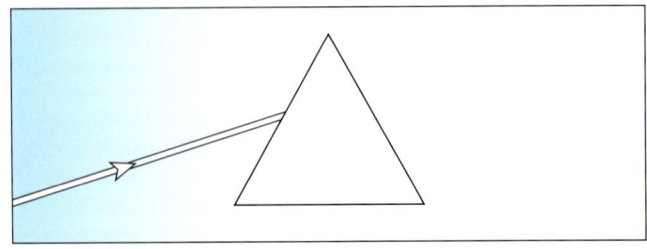

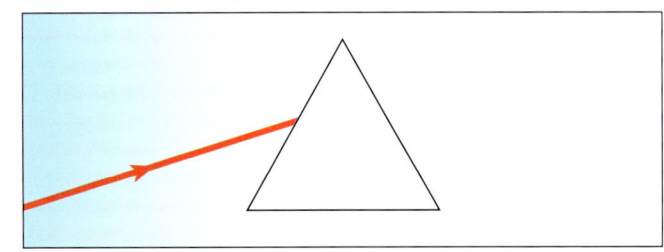

   b) Explain why the white light is "split up" by the prism.

   ....
   ....

2. **Radio waves, ultra violet, X-rays, microwaves, infra-red, gamma rays and light are all types of electromagnetic radiation. Their wavelengths are given in the table.**

	Radio waves	Ultra violet	X-rays	Infra-red	Microwaves	Gamma rays	Light
Wavelength (m)	1500	0.00000008	0.0000000009	0.00003	0.01	0.000000000004	0.000006

   Use the information given to complete the order of the electromagnetic spectrum.

   Shortest wavelength   Longest wavelength

   HIGHER/SPECIAL TIER

3. All E-M waves travel at a speed of 300 million m/s. Calculate the frequency of:

   a) Light. ....

   b) Radio waves. ....

4. The diagram below shows an X-ray tube used for producing X-rays

   a) X-rays are produced when very high speed electrons collide with a metal target.

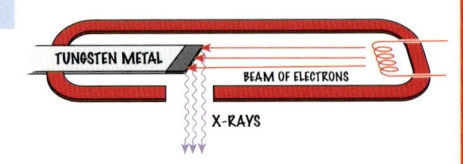

   (i) Why is there a vacuum inside the X-ray tube?

   ....

   (ii) A cooling liquid is used to cool down the target. Explain why the target gets hot.

   ....

   b) The X-ray tube has a lead shield around it except for the 'window'. Explain why?

   ....
   ....

USES AND DANGERS OF ELECTROMAGNETIC WAVES — Waves

1. X-rays are part of the electromagnetic spectrum. They can be useful to us.

   a) Explain the properties of X-rays that make them useful to us.

   b) X-rays can also be dangerous. Explain why X-rays can cause damage to human beings.

   c) Microwaves are also part of the electromagnetic spectrum.
      (i) Give one difference between X-rays and microwaves.

      (ii) Microwaves can be used for communication. State and explain another use for microwaves.

      (iii) Recently there has been a lot of concern about the use of mobile phones and its effect on people's health. Explain why microwaves can cause damage to human beings.

2. The table shows the main parts of the electromagnetic spectrum.

   a) Complete the table.

Radio			Light			

   b) Which type of electromagnetic radiation is used
      (i) to send information to and from satellites?
      (ii) in sunbeds to give a suntan?
      (iii) in remote controls for TVs and video recorders?
      (iv) with fluorescent lamps to security code electrical goods?

   c) Describe how long wavelength radio waves can be used to communicate over vast distances

   d) Gamma rays can be used to kill cancer cells. Gamma rays are also a danger to health. Explain why this is so.

SOUND — Waves

1. a) What type of wave is a sound wave?

   b) The picture shows "Jane the rocker" on her world tour.
      (i) Describe how the sound travels from her loudspeaker to the audience.

   c) During the sound check the sound engineer recorded a note from Jane's guitar. The trace on a CRO is shown in A. She then recorded another note, the trace on a CRO is shown in B.

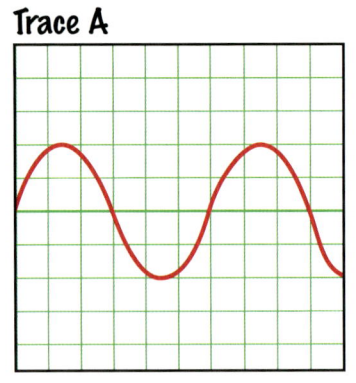

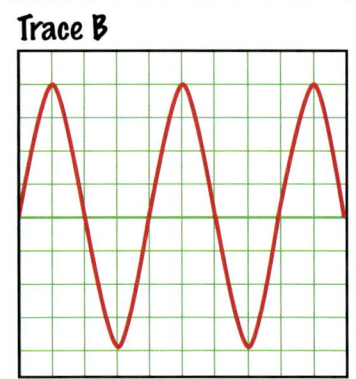

   Trace A   **Trace B**

      (i) Which note was the loudest? Explain your answer.

      (ii) Which note was of the higher pitch? Explain your answer.

   d) (i) Jane then played a note whose loudness and pitch were doubled compared to the note in Trace A. Sketch the trace of this note on trace A.

      (ii) Jane then played a note whose loudness is a quarter and pitch a half of the note in Trace B. Sketch the trace of this note on Trace B.

   e) (i) "Jane the rocker" claims "to play it loud and play it fast". The sound engineer measured the loudness to be equal to 120 decibels. Is Jane's claim to loudness true?

      (ii) Jane wants the sound engineer to "crank it up to 140 dB". What effect would this have on the audience?

2. The diagrams below show the traces on an oscilloscope screen

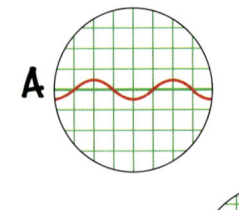

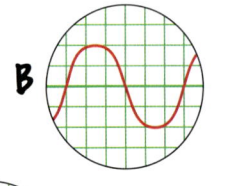

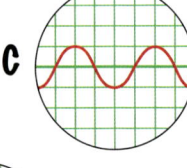

   A   B   C   Which of the traces A to E shows:

   D   E

   a) The quietest sound.
   b) The highest pitch.
   c) The loudest sound.
   d) The lowest pitch.

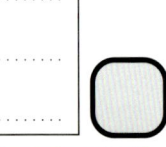

ULTRASOUND

• Waves

1. a) What is ultrasound?

   ....

   b) Pregnant women have ultrasound scans to check on the progress of the unborn baby
      (i) The image produced by ultrasound is not as clear as an image produced by X-rays. Why is ultrasound used for looking at unborn babies rather than X-rays?

      ....

   (ii) Why is it important to have a very narrow beam of ultrasound waves?

   ....

   (iii) Describe how ultrasound is used to produce an image of the developing baby.

   ....

2. Echo sounders can be used to locate submarines.

   a) Using the diagram to help you, explain how echo-sounders are used to locate the submarine.

   ....

3. Ultrasound can be used to detect flaws in metal. An arrangement for this is shown below.

   a) Which wave A or B would arrive at the receiver first? ....

   b) Explain how this arrangement is used to detect flaws.

   ....

4. Explain how ultra sound is used by dentists to remove plaque from teeth.

   ....

5. a) Describe how ultrasound can be used for cleaning watches

   ....

STRUCTURE OF THE EARTH AND SEISMIC WAVES • Waves

1. a) Use the information below to draw a fully labelled diagram showing the structure of the Earth.

Part of Earth	Distance from centre of Earth in cm
Inner Core	0.7
Outer Core	1.6
Mantle	3.1
Crust	3.2

b) If the scale used in your diagram is 1cm : 2000km. What is the radius of

(i) The Inner core? ....

(ii) The Earth? ....

HIGHER/SPECIAL TIER

2. The diagram shows how the speed of P waves change as they travel through the Earth.

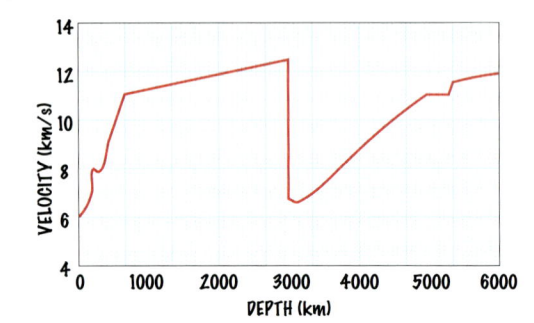

a) Explain why the speed of the waves falls at a depth of 3000km.

....

b) What evidence has the study of seismic waves given scientists about the structure of the Earth. Explain your answer.

....

3. The diagram shows the structure of the Earth. An earthquake occurs at point A on the Earth's surface. Two types of shock waves are produced by the earthquake P waves and S waves.

a) Complete the diagram to show the path of the P waves (in red) and S waves (in blue) through the earth.

b) State whether P waves or S waves or both will reach

(i) Station Y

....

(ii) Station Z

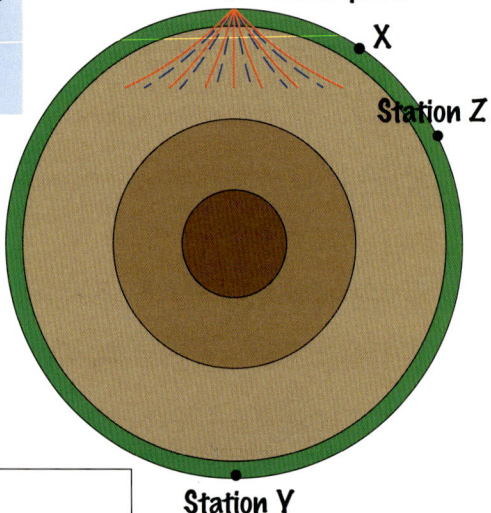

....

c) Explain your answer

....

d) Buildings at X were seen to vibrate up and down and then a few seconds later vibrate from side to side. Explain why this was so.

....

STRUCTURE OF THE ATOM — Radioactivity

1. The diagram below shows a simple model of a Lithium atom, Li. Lithium has an atomic number of 3 and a mass number of 7.

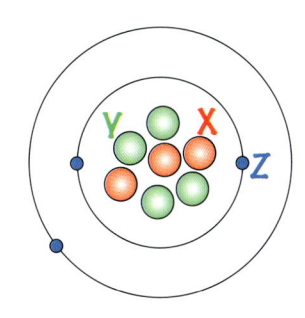

   a) Name each of the particles X, Y, Z.

   X = ... Y = ... Z = ...

   b) Complete the table.

Atomic Particle	Relative Mass	Relative Charge
Proton		
	1	
		-1

2. Complete the following table by writing in the missing figures.

Element	Copper	Silicon	Magnesium	Iron	Oxygen	Lead	Gold	Carbon	Neon	Calcium
Symbol	$^{64}_{29}Cu$	$^{28}_{14}Si$	$^{\ }_{\ }Mg$	$^{56}_{26}Fe$	$^{16}_{8}O$	$^{\ }_{82}Pb$	$^{197}_{79}Au$	$^{12}_{6}C$	$^{\ }_{\ }Ne$	$^{40}_{\ }Ca$
Mass Number			24							
Number of Protons			12							
Number of Neutrons						125			10	
Number of Electrons									10	20

3. Two isotopes of cobalt exists. Cobalt - 60 and Cobalt - 59 $^{60}_{27}Co$ and $^{59}_{27}Co$

   a) What is an isotope? ....

   b) For each isotope write down:

   (i) the number of protons   Cobalt - 60 = ...   Cobalt - 59 = ...

   (ii) the number of neutrons   Cobalt - 60 = ...   Cobalt - 59 = ...

   (i) the number of electrons   Cobalt - 60 = ...   Cobalt - 59 = ...

4. Uranium has three isotopes. $^{235}_{92}U$ $^{237}_{92}U$ $^{238}_{92}U$

   a) How is the nucleus of a uranium - 238 atom different to the nucleus of a uranium - 235 atom?

   ....

RADIOACTIVE DECAY — Radioactivity

1. a) What do we mean if we say a substance is radioactive?

   ....

   b) A teacher decided to do an experiment to find out which type(s) of radiation was emitted by a radioactive source.

   (i) Initially a reading was taken with the radioactive source absent. The Geiger counter gave a reading of 24 counts per minute. What is the significance of this reading?

   ....

   c) The source was then introduced and the experiment was set up as shown.

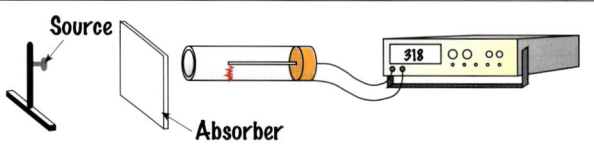

   Different absorbers were placed between the source and the Geiger counter. The radiation reaching the Geiger counter was measured for one minute. The results are shown opposite.

Absorber used	Average counts per minute
No absorber	1900
Card 1mm thick	1900
Aluminium 1mm thick	500
Lead 1cm thick	120

   (i) What type or types of radiation did the source emit? ....

   (ii) Explain your answer

   ....
   ....
   ....

   (iii) Why was the count-rate reduced to 120 counts per minute with 1cm of lead but not down as low as background levels?

   ....

2. Power station workers wear a special film badge to check how much radiation they have been exposed to. A diagram of the badge is shown opposite.

   a) Why is the photographic film wrapped in paper?

   ....

   b) What would happen to the photographic film on exposure to radiation?

   ....

   c) How could the film be used to find out how much radiation the person had been exposed to?

   ....

THE DECAY PROCESS — Radioactivity

HIGHER/SPECIAL TIER

1. Radioisotopes emit 3 types of radiation. For each type of radiation describe:

   (i) the nature of the radiation   (ii) how the radiation is emitted

   a) α particles (alpha)

   b) β particles (beta)

   c) γ rays (gamma)

2. The following radioisotopes decay by the emission of radiation. For each one complete the balanced equation.

   a) Californium: Cf to Curium: Cm by alpha decay

   $$^{241}_{98}Cf \longrightarrow \quad Cm \; + $$

   b) Iodine: I to Xenon: Xe by beta decay

   $$^{131}_{53}I \longrightarrow \quad Xe \; + $$

   c) Americium: Am to Neptunium: Np by alpha decay

   $$Am \longrightarrow ^{237}_{93}Np \; + $$

   d) Strontium: Sr to Yttrium: Y by beta decay

   $$Sr \longrightarrow ^{90}_{39}Y \; + $$

   e) Polonium: Po to Astatine: At by beta decay

   $$^{218}Po \longrightarrow \;_{85}At \; + $$

   f) Radium: Ra to Radon: Rn by alpha decay

   $$^{226}_{88}Ra \longrightarrow \quad Rn \; + $$

   g) Phosphorus: P to Sulphur: S by beta decay

   $$_{15}P \longrightarrow ^{32}S \; + $$

   (i) Which other type of radiation could also be emitted during the above decay processes.

G.C.S.E. Ref: Page 80   Lonsdale Science Revision Guides - Physics Double Award Higher/Special & Foundation Tiers

USES OF RADIOACTIVE ISOTOPES — Radioactivity

1. The diagram shows a method of controlling the thickness of steel at a steel mill. A radioactive source which emits γ rays is placed on one side of the steel and a radiation detector is placed on the other.

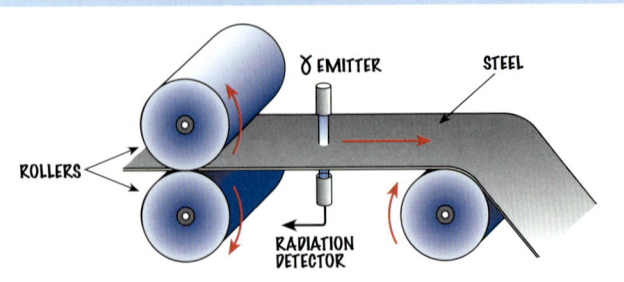

   a) How will the amount of radiation reaching the detector change as the steel gets thicker?

   b) What effect will this have on the distance the rollers are kept apart?

   c) Explain, in detail, why a radioisotope which emits α or β particles could not be used for this job

   d) Explain, in detail, why a radioisotope which emits γ rays is used for this job.

2. The graph shows how the count rate as detected by a Geiger counter changes with distance after a radioisotope had been injected into a pipe that was leaking at an oil refinery.

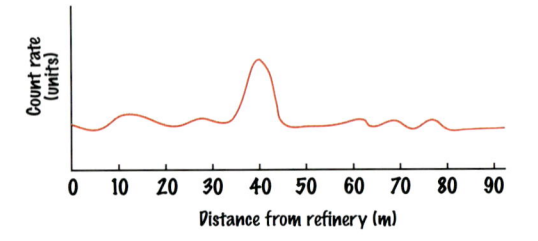

   a) What type of radiation should the radioisotope emit? Give reasons for your answer.

   b) Where would you expect to find the leak? Explain your answer.

   c) What type of half-life would you expect the tracer to have? Explain your answer.

3. Radiation can be used to sterilise medical instruments.

   a) What type of radiation would be used for this job?

   b) Why do the instruments become sterile.

   c) What is the advantage of sterilising the instruments this way compared to heating or chemical treatment?

EFFECT OF RADIATION ON LIVING ORGANISMS — Radioactivity

1. Radiation emitted from a radioactive material is often called "ionising radiation."

   a) Explain what is meant by the word "ionising"?

   b) Why is ionising radiation dangerous to humans?

2. Gamma rays are emitted by radioactive substances. Medically they can be helpful or harmful to humans.

   a) Explain how gamma rays can be helpful to humans.

   b) Explain how gamma rays can be harmful to humans.

3. The picture shows a worker at a nuclear plant.

   a) Name a suitable material for the protective screen.

   b) How does this screen help protect him from radiation?

   c) If the screen was not there what effect would each type of radiation have on him?

   α

   β

   γ

   d) It is very important that workers in the nuclear industry do not injest (breath in or eat) radioactive substances. What precautions can be taken to prevent this?

   e) What are the effects of each type of radiation on human cells if they do enter the body?

   α

   β

   γ

G.C.S.E. Ref: Page 82

HALF-LIFE

Radioactivity

HIGHER/SPECIAL TIER

1. An experiment was set up to calculate the half-life of a radioactive substance. Background radiation count rate was 30 counts per minute. With a radioisotope present the count rate was taken every five minutes for 20 minutes. The table below shows the results.

   a) Complete the table.

Time (min)	Count rate (counts per minute)	Corrected Count Rate
0	330	
5	180	
10	110	
15	75	
20	45	

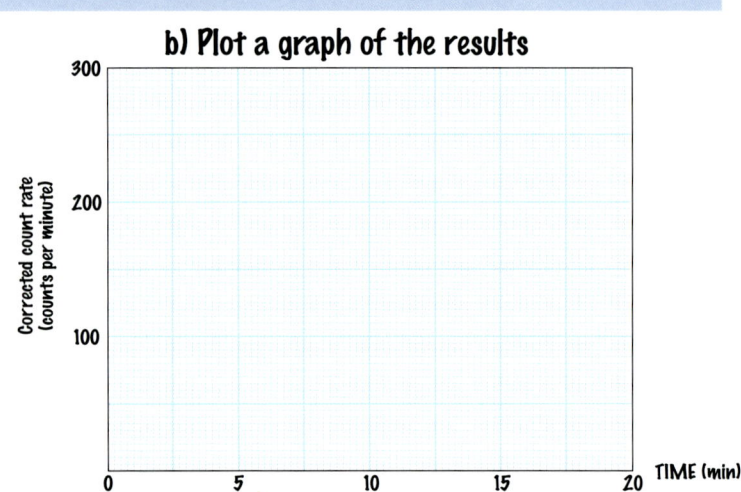

   b) Plot a graph of the results

   c) Use the information given to estimate the half-life of the substance.

   d) Use your graph to find out:
   (i) the count rate after 17 minutes =
   (ii) the time when the count rate was 160 counts per minute =

2. a) Americium-241 is used in smoke detectors. It has a half-life of 460 years.

   (i) Why is it important that americium-241 has a long half-life?

   (ii) How long would it take americium-241 to decrease to one eighth of its original number of radioactive atoms?

   b) Iodine-138 is a radioactive substance. It has a half-life of 6 seconds. A Geiger counter is used and the corrected count rate for a sample of iodine-138 is found to be 2000 counts/minute. How long will it take for the count rate to decrease to 125 counts/minute?

   c) The relative amounts of potassium-40 and argon in a sample of igneous rock can be used to date the rock. A rock sample contains 7 times as many argon atoms compared to potassium atoms.

   (i) What fraction of the original potassium is left in the rock assuming there was no argon present to begin with?

   (ii) The half-life of potassium-40 is 1300 million years. Calculate the age of the rock.

NUCLEAR FISSION

Radioactivity

HIGHER/SPECIAL TIER

1. The diagram represents the process called nuclear fission.

   a) What do each of the following parts of the diagram represent?

   [_____]

   [_____]

   [_____]

   b) Explain as fully as you can:
      (i) How the fission of uranium atoms takes place in a nuclear reactor.

      [_____]

      (ii) How this leads to a chain reaction.

      [_____]

      (iii) How the chain reaction is controlled.

      [_____]

   c) Barium and kryton are formed as a result of the fission process. These are <u>radioactive</u> <u>isotopes</u> with long <u>half-lives</u>. Explain the underlined terms

      (i) radioactive [_____]

      (ii) isotopes [_____]

      (iii) half-life [_____]

2. A nuclear reactor core has 1200 uranium rods. Each rod can produce a total of 9×10^{13} Joules of energy.

   a) What is the total amount of energy that the rods can produce.

   [_____]

   b) If the reactor core produces energy at a rate of 2000MW, calculate how long the fuel will last for in years.

   [_____]

G.C.S.E. Ref: Page 84 — Lonsdale Science Revision Guides - Physics Double Award Higher/Special & Foundation Tiers

THE SOLAR SYSTEM

1. There are nine planets in our solar system.

   a) Name two planets that have a shorter period of orbit around the Sun compared to the Earth.

   (i) .... (ii) ....

   b) Why is their period of orbit less than the Earths?

   ....

   c) Venus is often seen to be shining in the early evening sky. Why can we see Venus?

   ....

   d) The period of orbit of Mars is about 15 times less than that of Saturn. Give a reason for this.

   ....

   e) The pictures show the night sky at the same time on two different nights, a few weeks apart. They show a planet and some stars. For each picture name which letter represents the planet. Explain your answer.

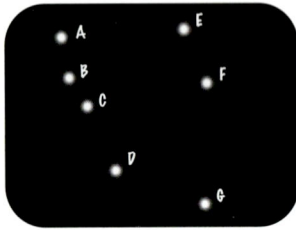

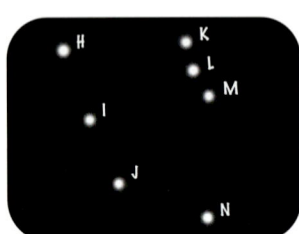

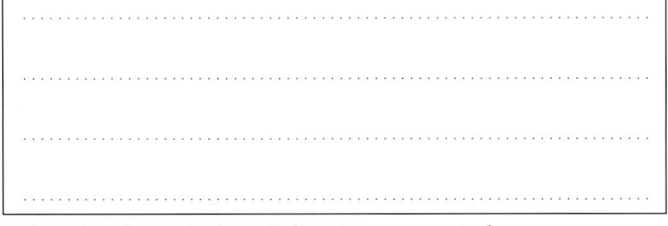

   ....

   f) The picture shows the night sky as viewed from the Earth and the night sky viewed from the same place on Earth six months later. Explain why the two views are different.

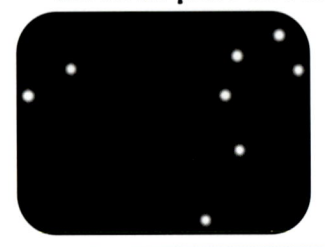

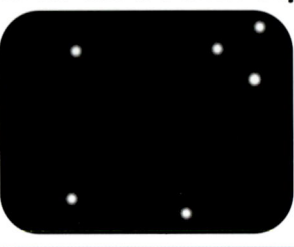

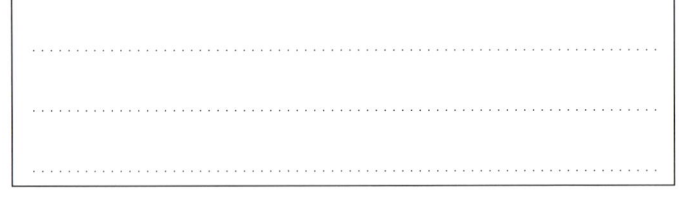

   ....

2. The diagram shows the path of a comet around the Sun

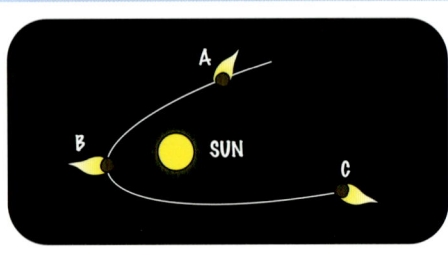

   a) Explain why the comet has a tail.

   ....

   b) Why does the tail always point away from the Sun?

   ....

   c) Explain why comets are not seen very often.

   ....

   d) Comets are only seen for a short time, explain why this is so.

   ....

   e) What are asteroids?

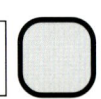

   ....

THE EARTH

The Solar System

1. The drawing shows the Earth

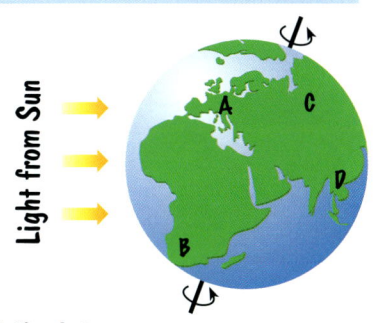

   a) State which place A, B, C or D is

   (i) experiencing daytime ....

   (ii) experiencing night-time ....

   (iii) experiencing Summer ....

   (iv) experiencing Winter ....

   b) Explain your answers.

2. The diagram shows the path of the Sun across the sky on the 21 September in the UK. On the diagram draw the path of the Sun across the sky on

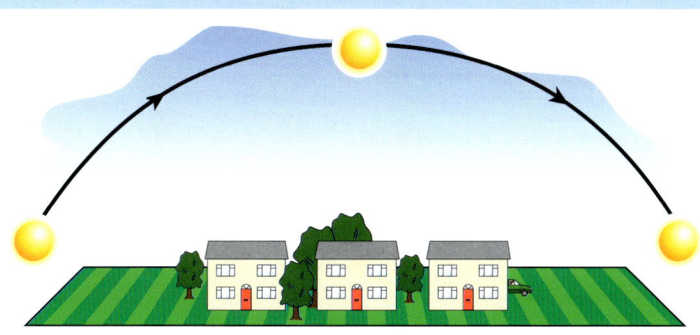

   a) 21 December, label it D.
   b) 21 June, label it J.
   c) On which of these days is.

   (i) the length of daytime the longest? ....
   (ii) the length of night-time the longest? ....

   (iii) Explain your answers.

3. James was camping. He could not sleep. He looked up at the sky at 10pm, 1am and 3am. The diagrams show what he saw.

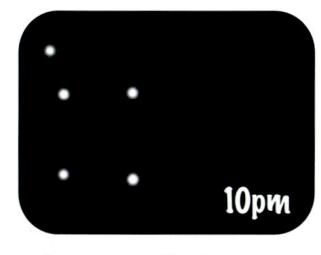

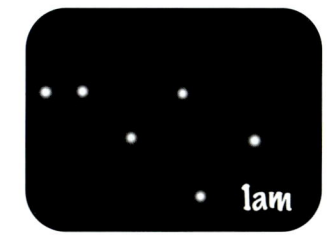

   10pm   1am   3am

   Explain why the constellation appears to move across the night sky.

4. Explain the different seasons.

G.C.S.E. Ref: Page 88

THE MOON

The Solar System

1. The diagram shows the Moon in orbit around the Earth. Rays of light coming from the Sun are also drawn on the diagram. The diagram is not drawn to scale.

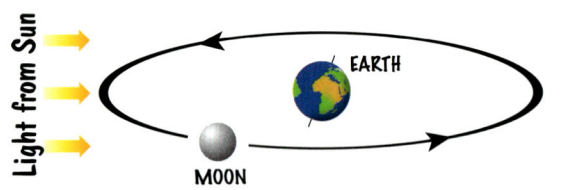

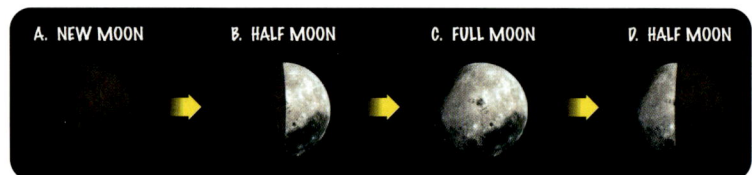

   a) The pictures A, B, C and D show how the Moon looks from the Earth at various times in its orbit.
      (i) Each picture represents a phase of the Moon. Mark on the Moon's orbit, the positions at which the Moon appears to look like at A, B, C and D.

      (ii) How many days are there between one half Moon and the next half Moon?

2. The diagram shows the effect of the Moon's gravitational pull on the oceans and seas of the Earth. The Earth has been treated as a perfect sphere completely covered with a layer of water.

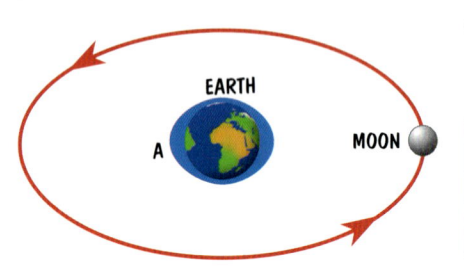

   (the diagram is not drawn to scale).

   a) Explain how tides are produced.

   b) Why is there a high tide at point A?

3. Tides are also influenced by the Sun. The picture below shows the Earth, Moon and Sun.

   (the diagram is not drawn to scale).

   a) On the diagram mark with an X two positions of the Moon which would produce the largest tides.

   b) On the diagram mark with a Y two positions of the Moon which would produce the smallest tides.

   HIGHER/SPECIAL TIER

   c) Explain how the gravitational pull of the Sun and Moon on the Earth produce tides of different sizes throughout the year.

SATELLITES
The Solar System

1. Some Satellites are put into orbit above the Earth at a height of **35800** kilometres and a speed of **3** kilometres per second. This gives them an orbit time of **24** hours.

   a) What is the name given to this type of orbit?

   b) Suggest a use for this type of orbit.
      Explain why this type of orbit is suitable for this use.

2. The diagram shows a Satellite that orbits the Earth once every ninety minutes.

   a) (i) What is the name of the force acting on the satellite?

   (ii) What is the direction of this force?

   b) What is the name given to this type of orbit?

   c) Suggest a use for this type of orbit. Explain why this orbit is suitable for this use.

3. Satellites can be put into orbit as 'navigation beacons'. Suggest which type of orbit should be used and explain your choice.

4. The Hubble space telescope is in orbit around the Earth. Why should this telescope out perform telescopes on Earth which are much larger?

5. Recent disasters such as Earthquakes require a rapid response. Satellites can help with this response. Explain how satellites help with response to disasters.

G.C.S.E. Ref: Page 90 — Lonsdale Science Revision Guides - Physics Double Award Higher/Special & Foundation Tiers

GRAVITATIONAL FORCES — The Solar System

HIGHER/SPECIAL TIER

1. Satellites carry out many useful functions. They need to be launched into orbit around the Earth.

   a) What is the name of the force that keeps an object moving in a circular path?

   b) This force is provided by the gravitational pull of the Earth. On the diagram draw an arrow to show the direction of this force on the satellite.

   c) The satellite is launched using a rocket. Explain in detail how a rocket accelerates.

   d) Why is it necessary for a rocket to accelerate to a very high speed when carrying a satellite to its orbit?

   e) What would happen if the rocket could not reach a high enough speed?

2. The diagram shows two planets. They both have the same mass, M.

   a) Mark on the diagram the directions of the pull force acting on each planet.

   b) Planet Z is twice as far away from planet X compared to planet Y and in the opposite direction. If planet X exerts a pull force of value F on planet Y, what pull force would it exert on planet Z? Explain your answer.

   c) Two other planets A and B are the same distance apart as planets X and Y but each has a mass of 4M. Describe and explain how the pull force between A and B will be different to the pull force between X and Y.

   d) Two other planets P and Q have a mass of 8M and 2M respectively. At what distance apart, compared to X and Y do they need to be to have a pull force between them of F?

STARS

The Solar System

1. **a) Describe how stars like our Sun are formed.**

b) How are planets formed?

HIGHER/SPECIAL TIER

2. Our Sun is currently going through a stable period in its life cycle.

Describe the forces at work in the Sun during this stable period.

3. **a)** The two flow diagrams show the cycle of change which occurs when a star dies.
Each circle shows what is formed at the end of each change.
Complete each circle in the cycle by using the following words:

SUPERNOVA   RED GIANT   BLACK DWARF   RED SUPERGIANT   NEBULA   WHITE DWARF

STARS THE SIZE OF OUR SUN

STARS MUCH BIGGER THAN OUR SUN

Stage A

Stage B

Stage C

b) Explain what effect gravity has on Stage A?

c) Explain what happens during Stage B?

d) Explain what happens during Stage C?

G.C.S.E. Ref: Page 92   Lonsdale Science Revision Guides - Physics Double Award Higher/Special & Foundation Tiers   75

STARS, GALAXIES AND THE UNIVERSE — The Solar System

1. a) Rewrite the following in order of size, starting with the smallest.
   Universe, Planet, Galaxy, Solar system, Star.

   b) The nearest star to our solar system is Alpha Centauri which is 4.3 light years away.
      (i) What is a light year?

      (ii) Why are light years used as a measure of distance in astronomy?

HIGHER/SPECIAL TIER

2. The picture shows a spectra from our sun and two other different stars.

   (Spectra labelled SUN, STAR A, STAR B — RED END OF SPECTRUM on the left)

   Each of the lines represents a particular wavelength.
   a) What does the spectrum of Star A tell us about its movement?

   b) What does the spectrum of star B tell us about its movement?

   c) Explain how the evidence from the spectra above supports the 'Big Bang' theory of the origin of the Universe.

   d) The expansion of the Universe is slowing down.
      Suggest what might happen to the Universe in the future.

3. Complete the following crossword on stars, galaxies and the universe

   (Crossword grid with letters S, R, S, B, A, Y shown as hints)

NOTES

NOTES

NOTES

NOTES